EASY PIANO

GEORGE GERSHWIN

T0066249

ISBN 978-1-4950-0736-1

Visit Hal Leonard Online at **www.halleonard.com**

Explore the entire family of Hal Leonard products and resources

World headquarters, contact:
Hal Leonard
7777 West Bluemound Road
Milwaukee, WI 53213
Email: info@halleonard.com

In Europe, contact:
Hal Leonard Europe Limited
Dettingen Way
Bury St. Edmunds, Suffolk, IP33 3YB
Email: info@halleonardeurope.com

In Australia, contact:
Hal Leonard Australia Pty. Ltd.
4 Lentara Court
Cheltenham, Victoria, 3192 Australia
Email: info@halleonard.com.au

BIDIN' MY TIME

from GIRL CRAZY

Music and Lyrics by GEORGE GERSHWIN
and IRA GERSHWIN

Some fel - lers love to "Tip - Toe Thru' the

Tu - lips;" _____ some fel - lers go on

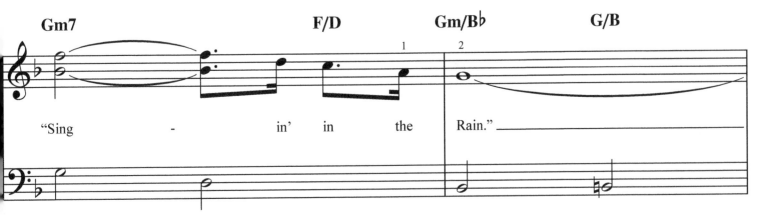

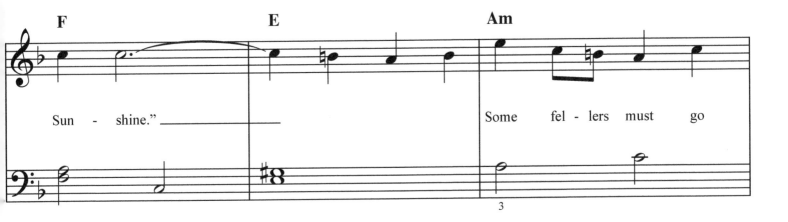

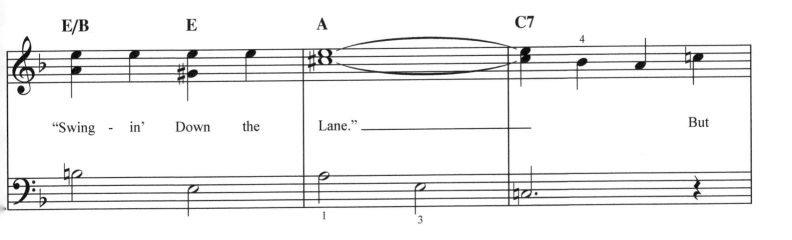

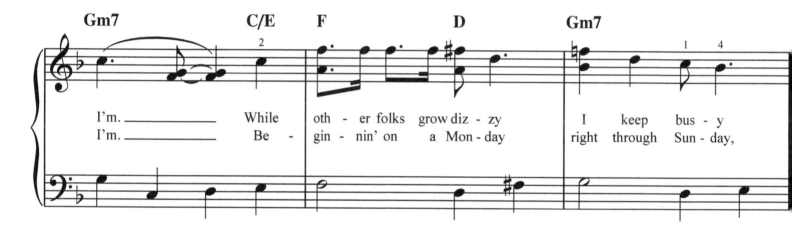

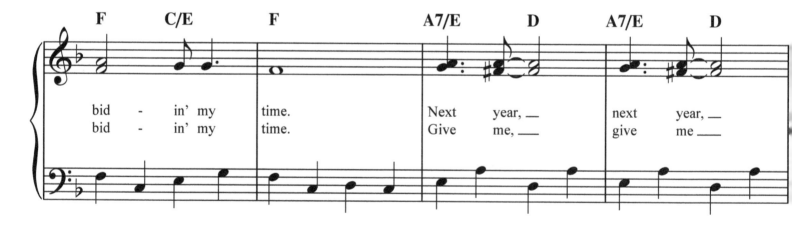

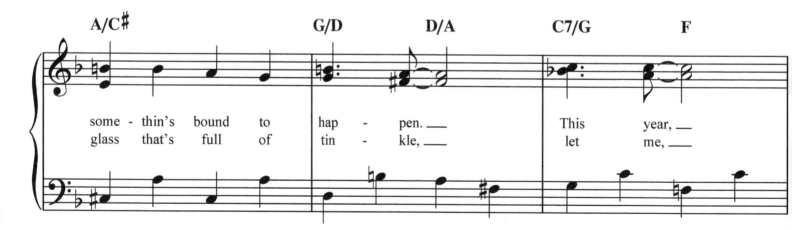

this year, ___ | I'll just keep on nap - pin' ___ and
let me ___ | dream like Rip Van Win - kle. ___

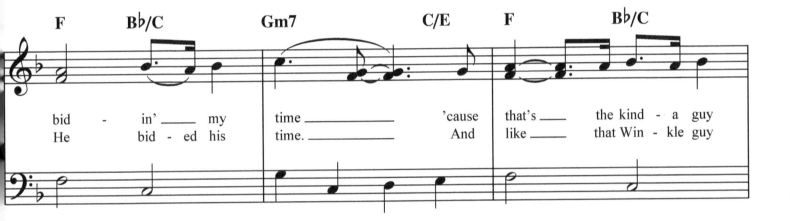

bid - in' ___ my | time ___ 'cause | that's ___ the kind - a guy
He bid - ed his | time. ___ And | like ___ that Win - kle guy

I'm. ___ | There's | no re - gret - tin' | when I'm set - tin',
I'm ___ | chas - in' 'way flies, | how the day flies,

bid - in' my | time.
bid - in' my | time.

EMBRACEABLE YOU

from CRAZY FOR YOU

Music and Lyrics by GEORGE GERSHWIN
and IRA GERSHWIN

Whimsically

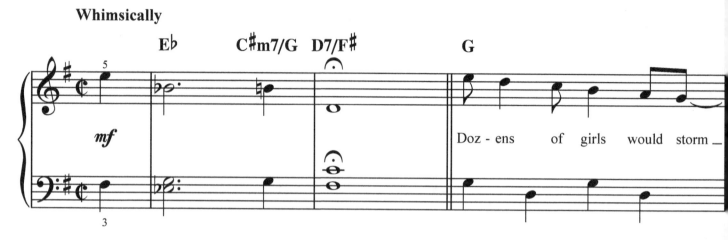

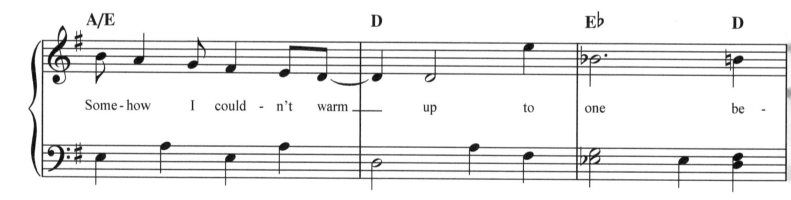

What kept my love-life lean? My in-tu-i-tion told___

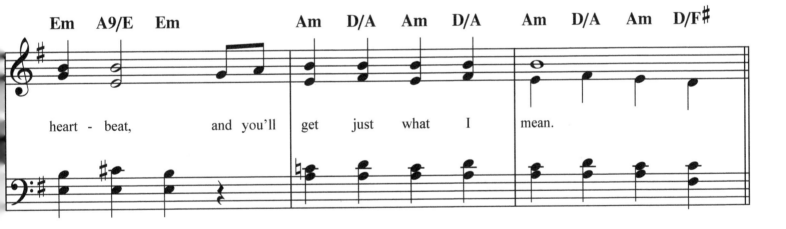

___ me you'd come on the scene. La-dy, lis-ten to the rhy-thm of my

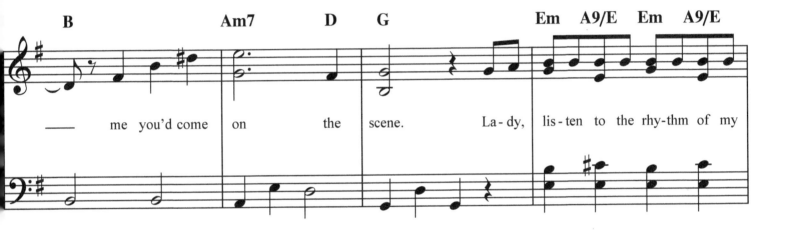

heart-beat, and you'll get just what I mean.

Em-brace me, my sweet em-brace - a-ble you! ___

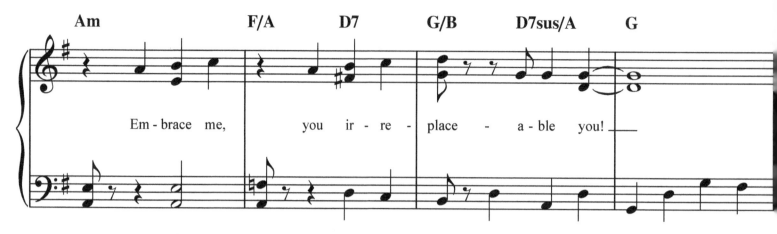

Em - brace me, you ir - re - place - a - ble you!

Just one look at you, my heart grew tip - sy in me;

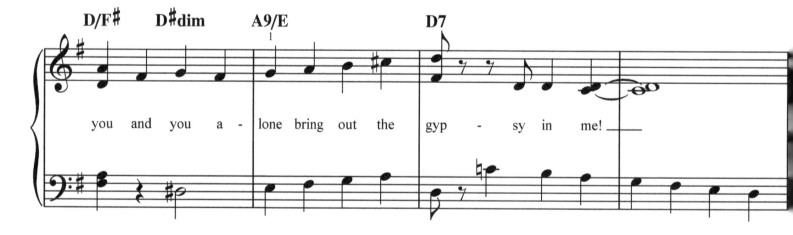

you and you a - lone bring out the gyp - sy in me!

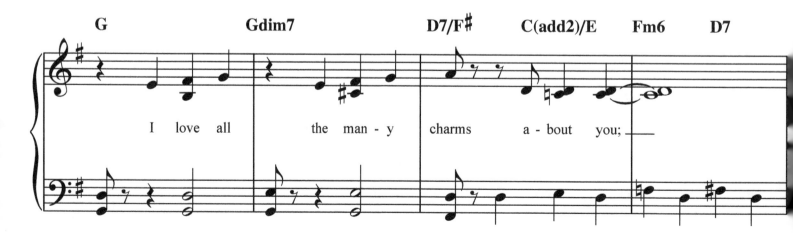

I love all the man - y charms a - bout you;

11

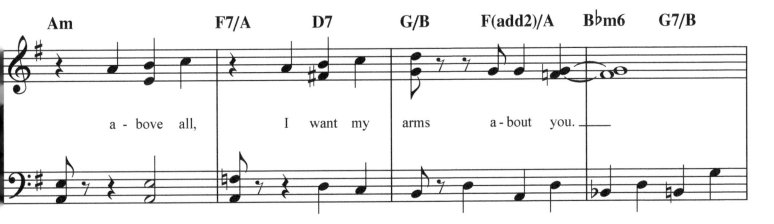

a - bove all,   I want my   arms   a - bout you. __

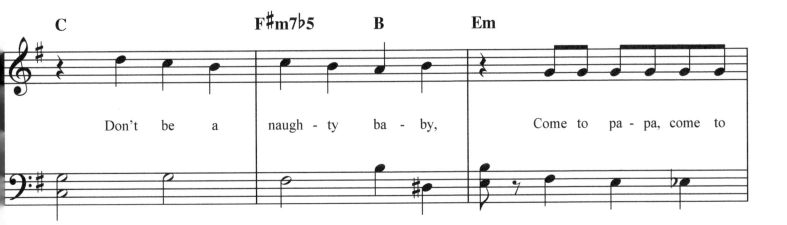

Don't be a   naugh - ty ba - by,   Come to pa - pa, come to

pa - pa, do!   My sweet em - brace - a - ble

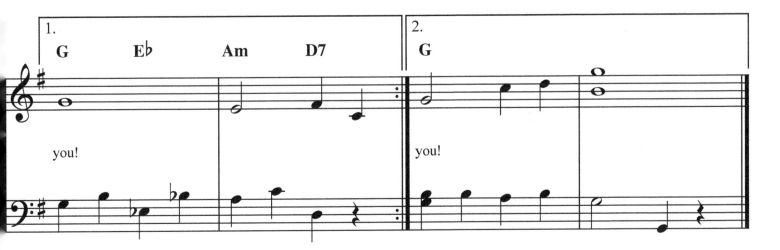

you!   you!

ISN'T IT A PITY?

from PARDON MY ENGLISH

Music and Lyrics by GEORGE GERSHWIN
and IRA GERSHWIN

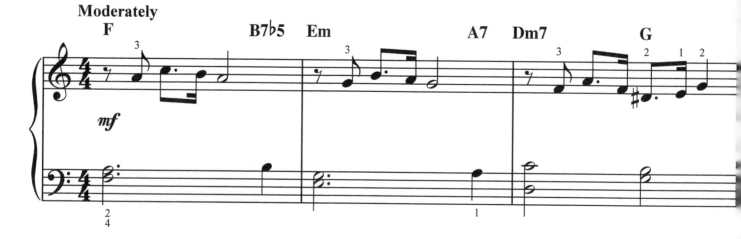

Why did I wan-der
While you were flit-ting

here and there and yon-der,
I was bus-y knit-ting,

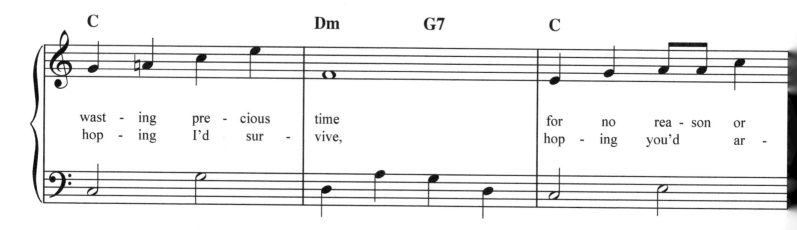

wast - ing pre - cious
hop - ing I'd sur -

time
vive,

for no rea - son or
hop - ing you'd ar -

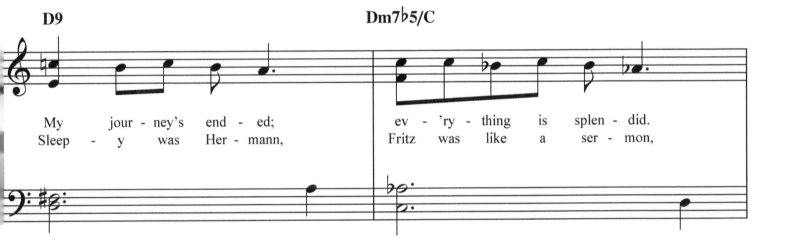

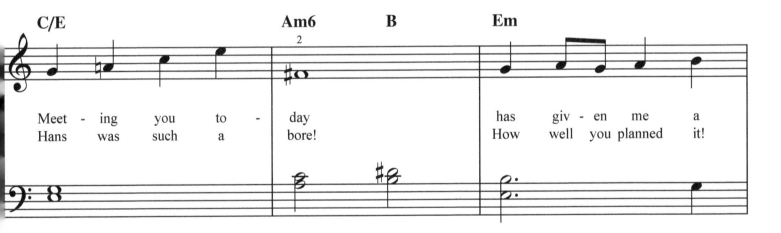

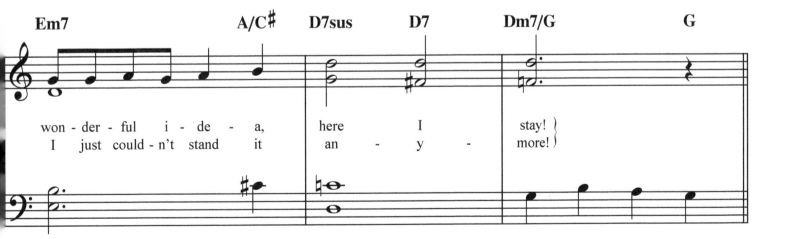

14

Not fast, with expression

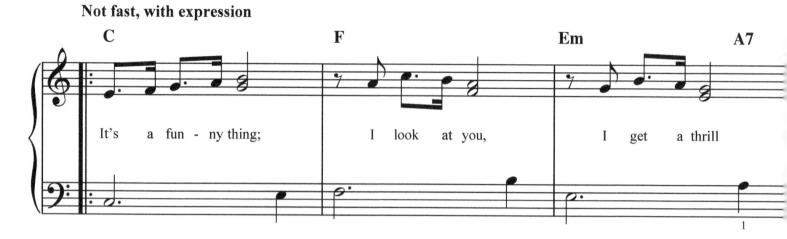

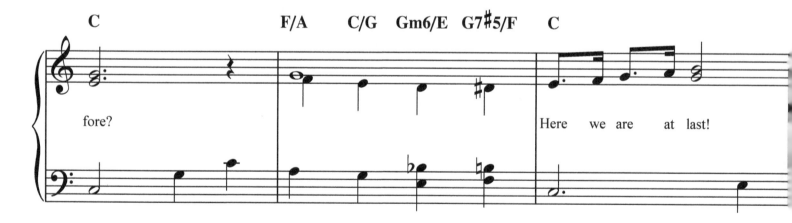

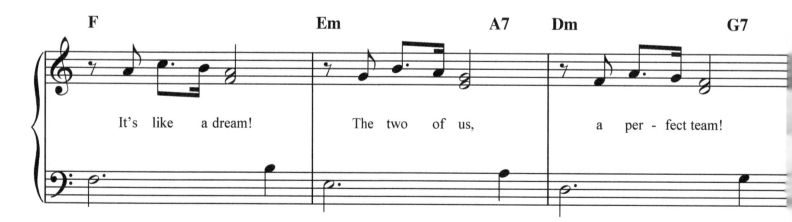

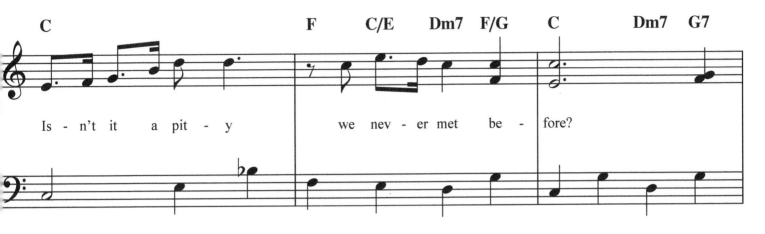

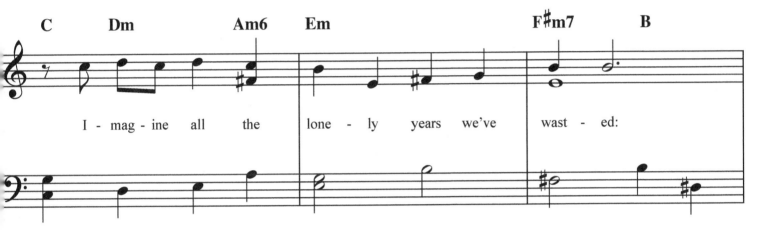

FASCINATING RHYTHM
from RHAPSODY IN BLUE

Music and Lyrics by GEORGE GERSHWIN
and IRA GERSHWIN

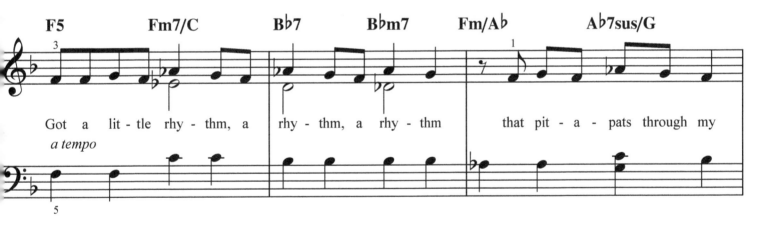

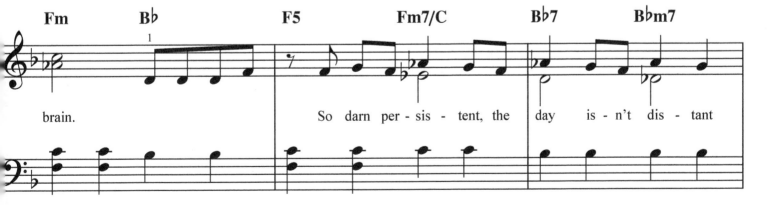

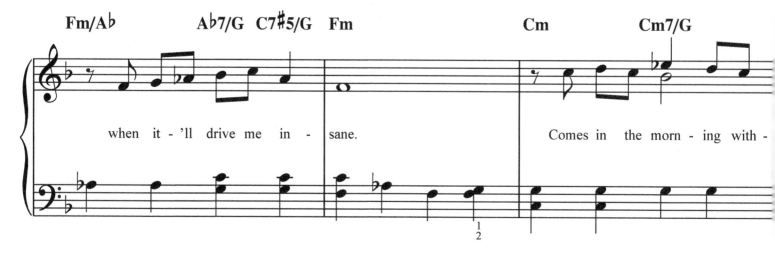

when it-'ll drive me in - sane. Comes in the morn - ing with -

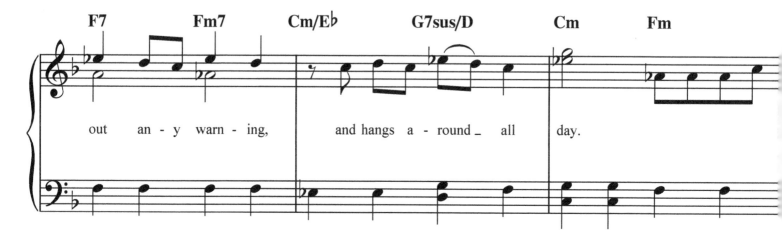

out an - y warn - ing, and hangs a - round __ all day.

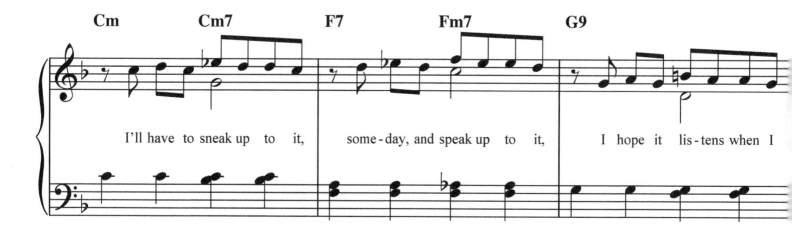

I'll have to sneak up to it, some - day, and speak up to it, I hope it lis - tens when I

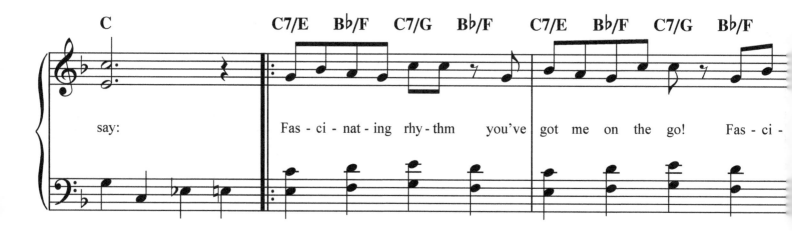

say: Fas - ci - nat - ing rhy - thm you've got me on the go! Fas - ci -

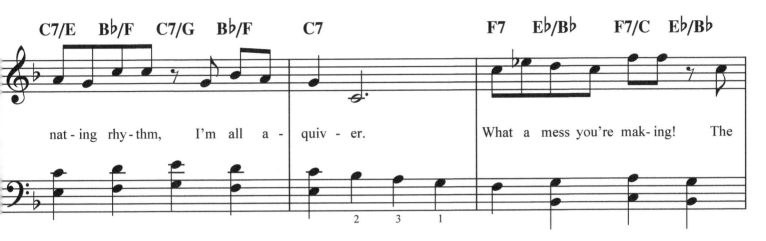

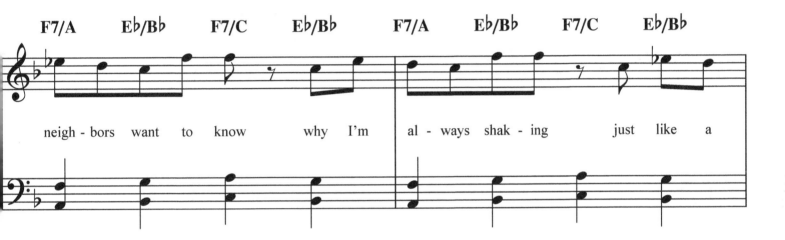

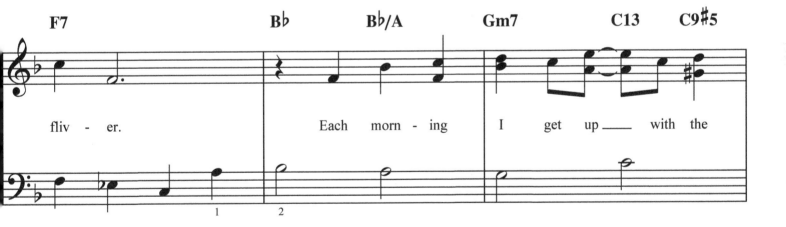

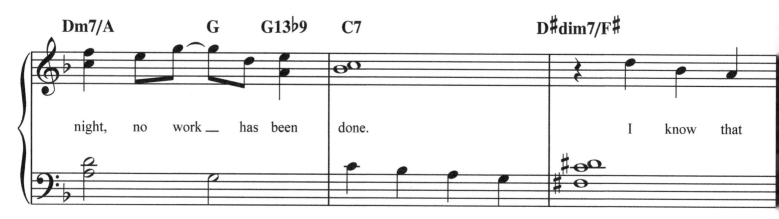

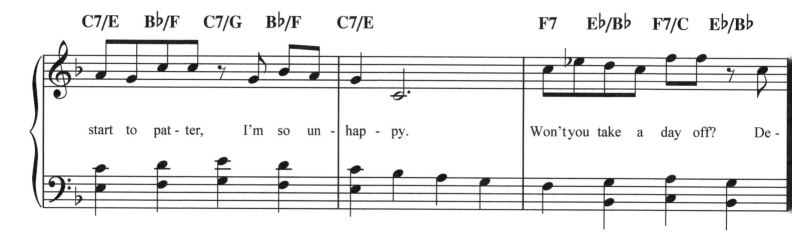

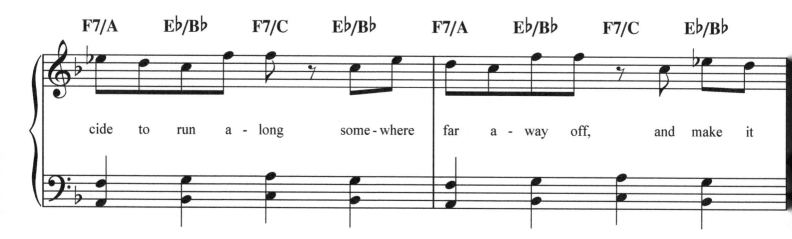

snap - py!   Oh, how I   long to be ____ the man

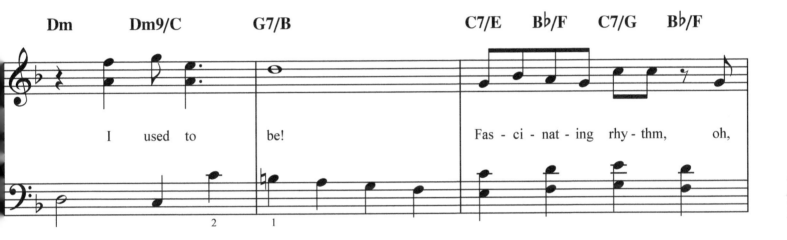

I used to   be!   Fas - ci - nat - ing rhy - thm,   oh,

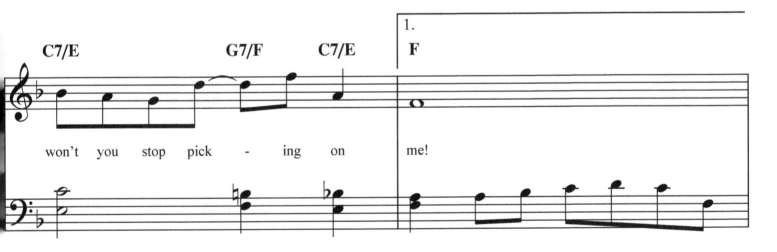

won't you stop pick - ing on   me!

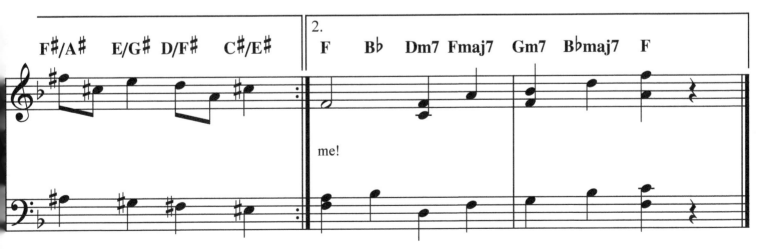

me!

FOR YOU, FOR ME FOR EVERMORE

Music and Lyrics by GEORGE GERSHWIN
and IRA GERSHWIN

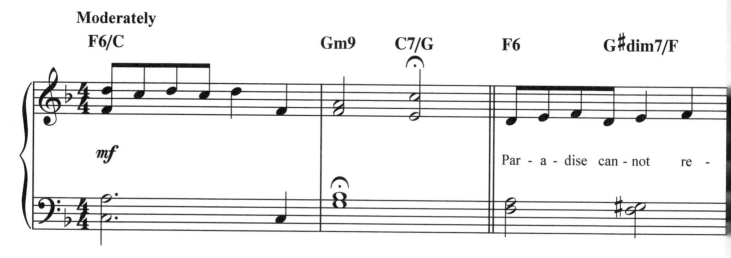

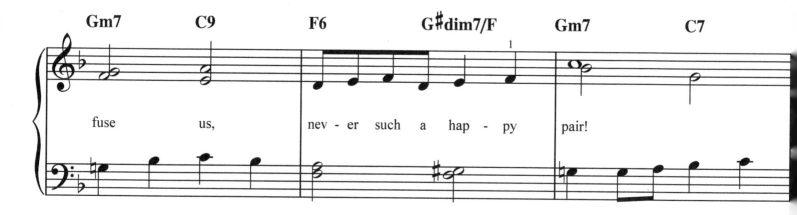

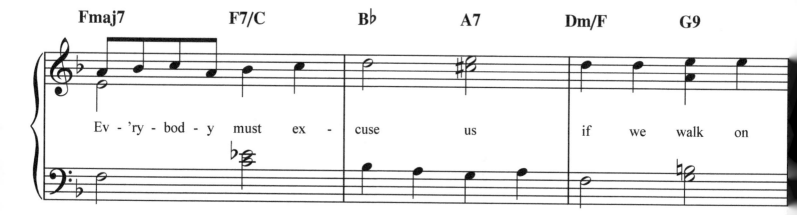

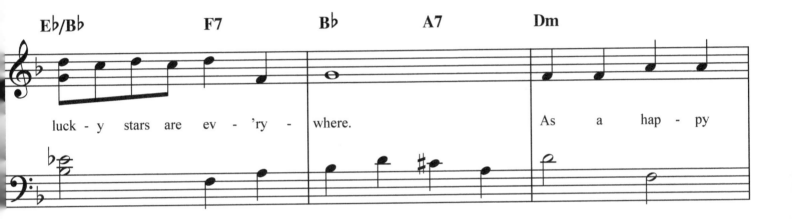

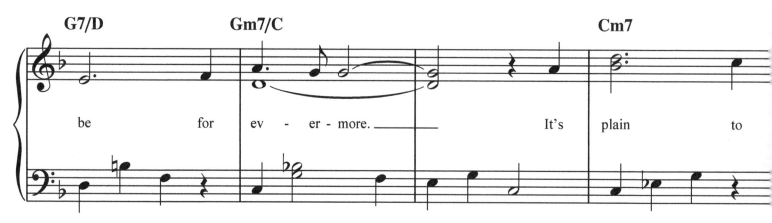

be for ev - er - more. _____ It's plain to

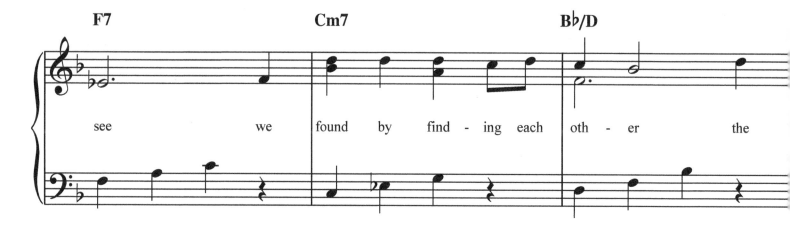

see we found by find - ing each oth - er the

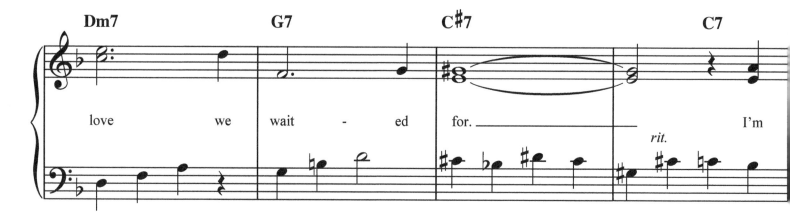

love we wait - ed for. _____ I'm

rit.

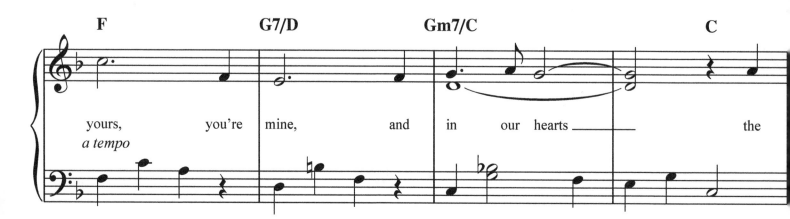

yours, you're mine, and in our hearts _____ the

a tempo

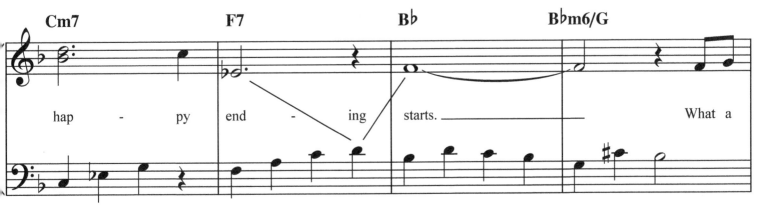

hap - py end - ing starts. _____ What a

love - ly world this world will be, with a world of love in

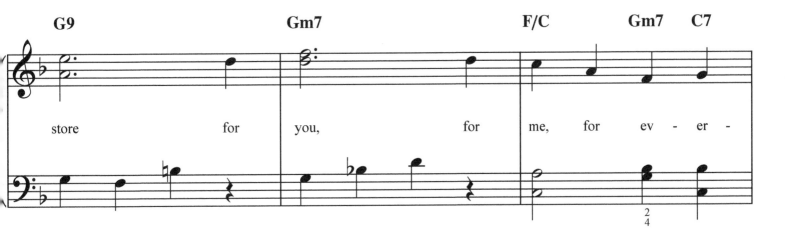

store for you, for me, for ev - er -

more! _____ For more! _____

HE LOVES AND SHE LOVES

from FUNNY FACE

Music and Lyrics by GEORGE GERSHWIN
and IRA GERSHWIN

Moderately

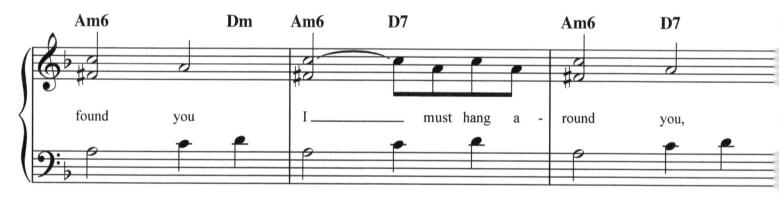

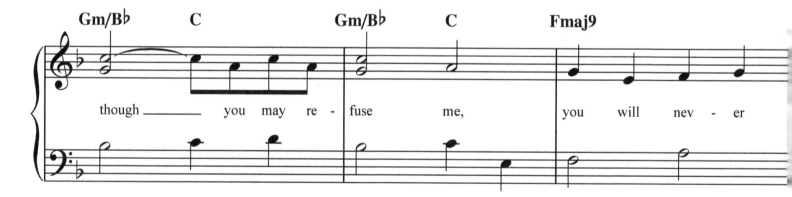

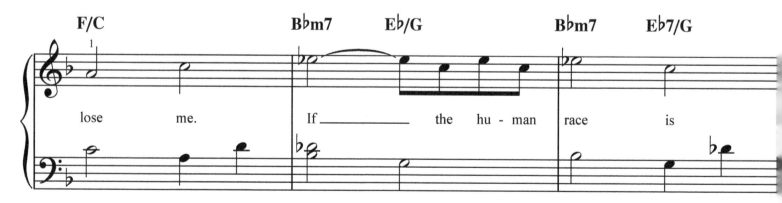

full _____ of hap - py fac - es, it's be - cause they

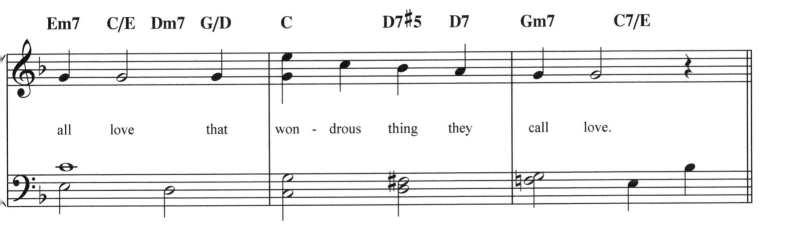

all love that won - drous thing they call love.

Slowly, with sentiment

He loves and she loves and they love, so

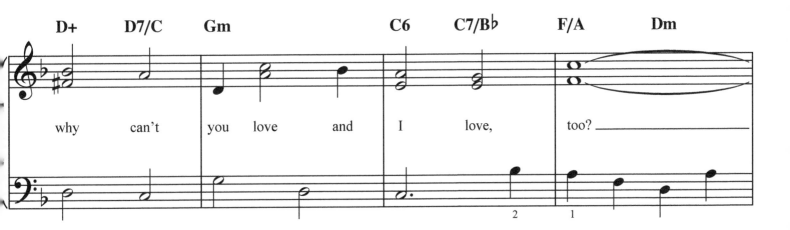

why can't you love and I love, too? _____

28

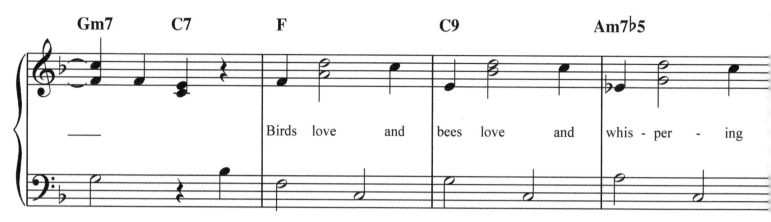

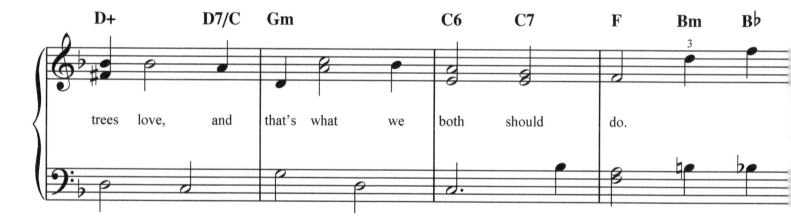

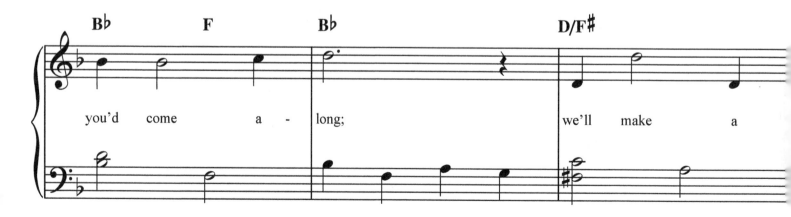

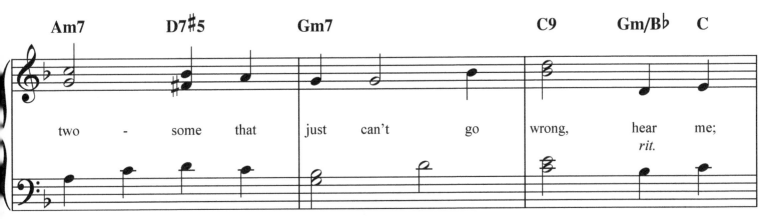

two - some that just can't go wrong, hear me;
rit.

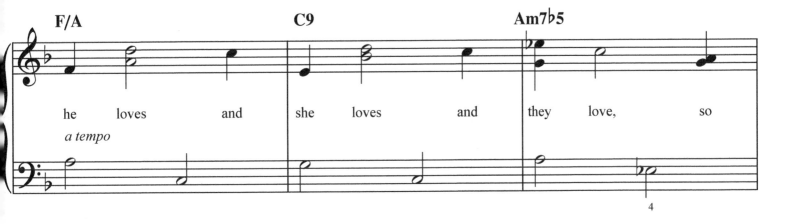

he loves and she loves and they love, so
a tempo

won't you love me as I love
why can't you love me and I love,

1.
you?

2.
too?

I GOT PLENTY O' NUTTIN'

from PORGY AND BESS ®

Music and Lyrics by GEORGE GERSHWIN,
DuBOSE and DOROTHY HEYWARD and IRA GERSHWIN

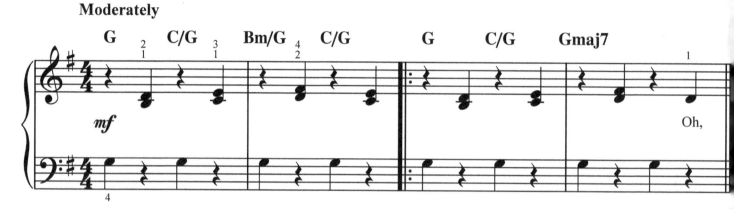

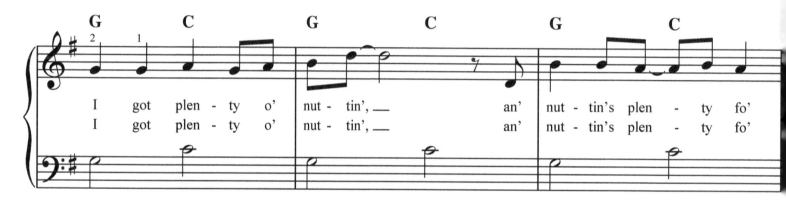

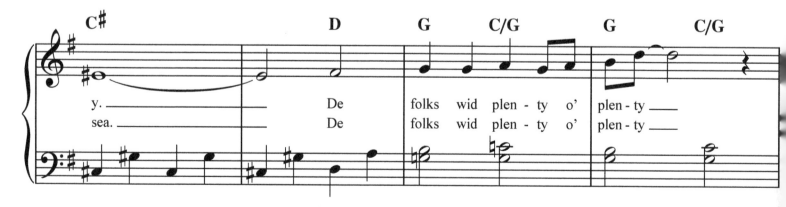

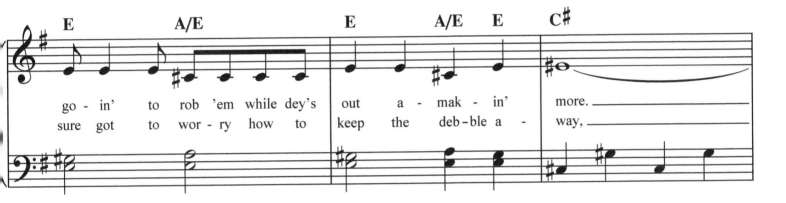

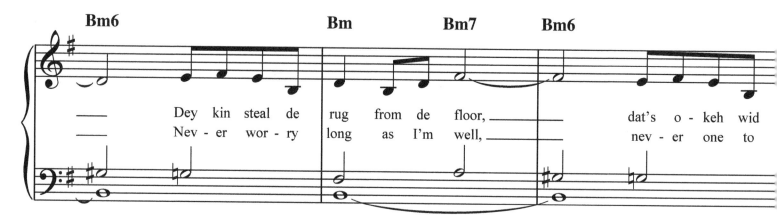

Dey kin steal de rug from de floor, ___ dat's o - keh wid
Nev - er wor - ry long as I'm well, ___ nev - er one to

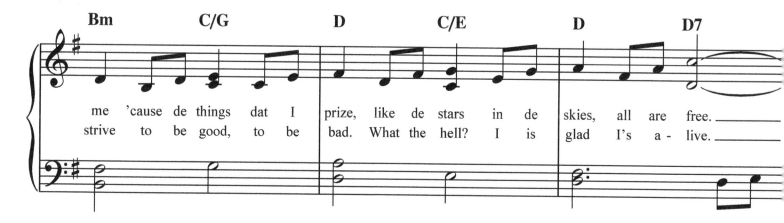

me 'cause de things dat I prize, like de stars in de skies, all are free. ___
strive to be good, to be bad. What the hell? I is glad I's a - live. ___

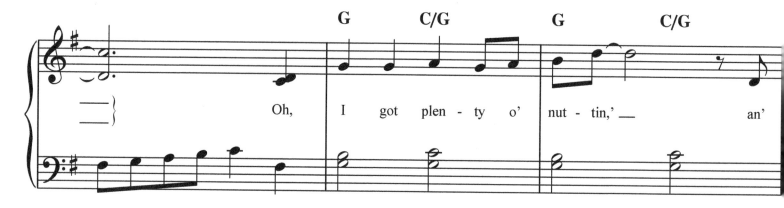

Oh, I got plen - ty o' nut - tin,' ___ an'

nut - tin's plen - ty fo' me. I got my gal, got my song, got

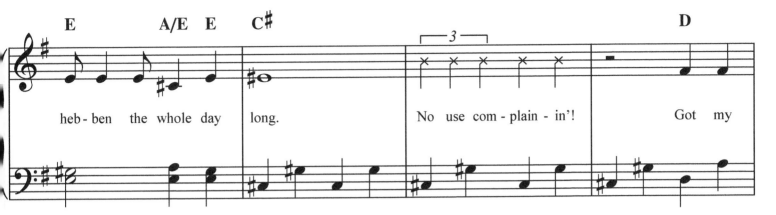

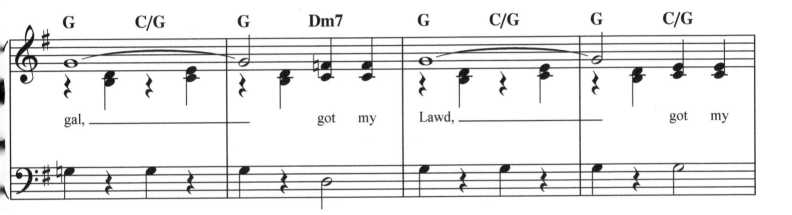

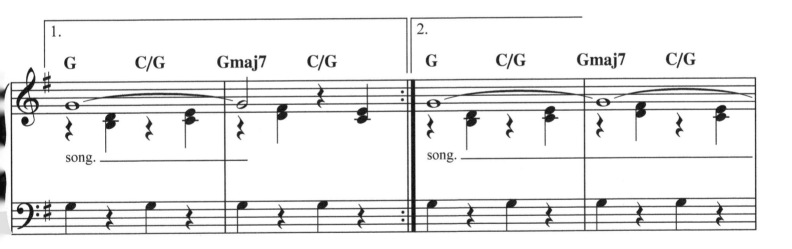

IT AIN'T NECESSARILY SO

from PORGY AND BESS ®

Music and Lyrics by GEORGE GERSHWIN,
DuBOSE and DOROTHY HEYWARD and IRA GERSHWIN

Moderately, with humor

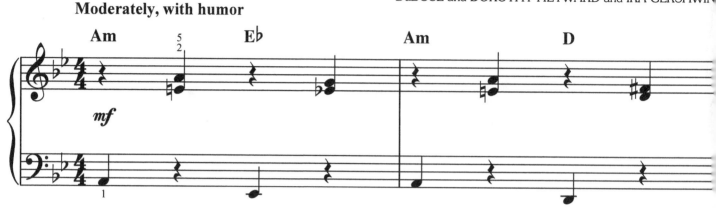

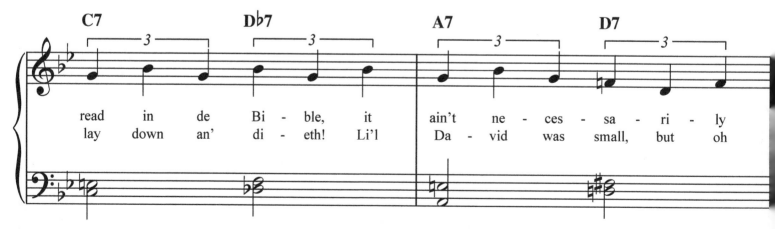

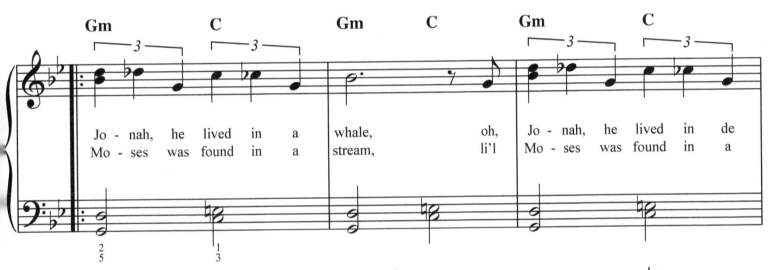

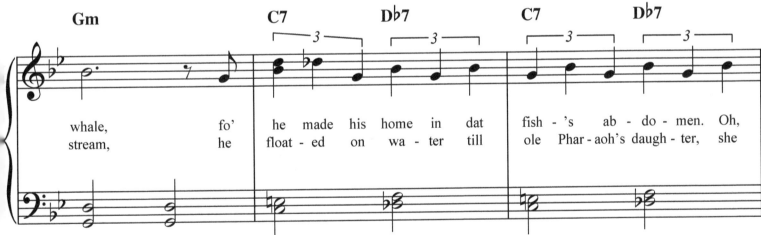

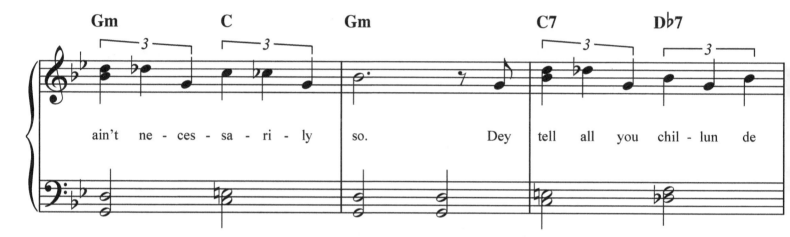

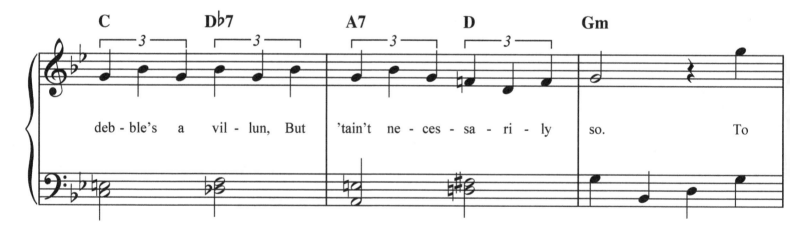

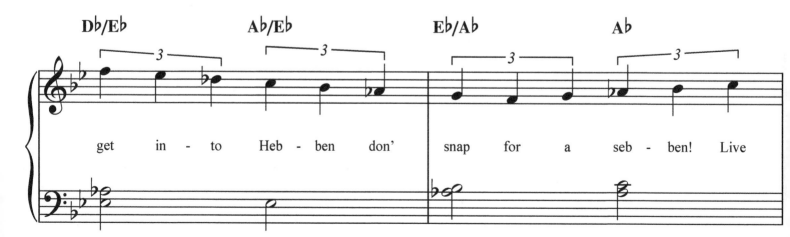

37

clean! Don' have no fault. Oh, I takes dat gos-pel when-

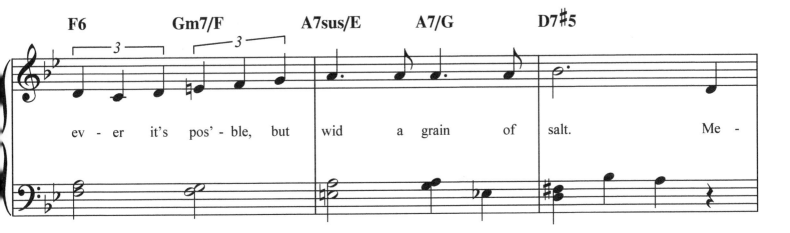

ev - er it's pos'- ble, but wid a grain of salt. Me -

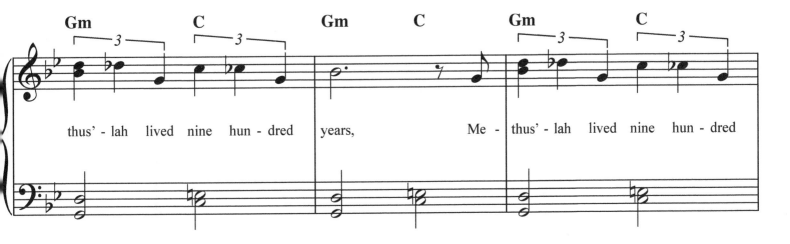

thus'- lah lived nine hun-dred years, Me - thus'- lah lived nine hun-dred

years, but who calls dat liv - in' when no gal 'll give in to

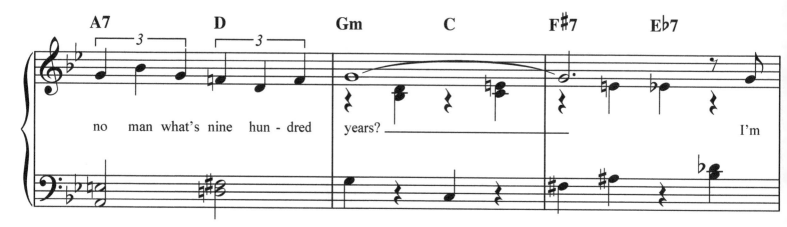

no man what's nine hun- dred years? _____ I'm

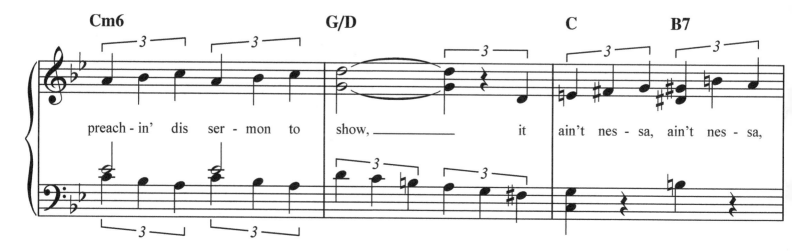

preach-in' dis ser-mon to show, _____ it ain't nes - sa, ain't nes - sa,

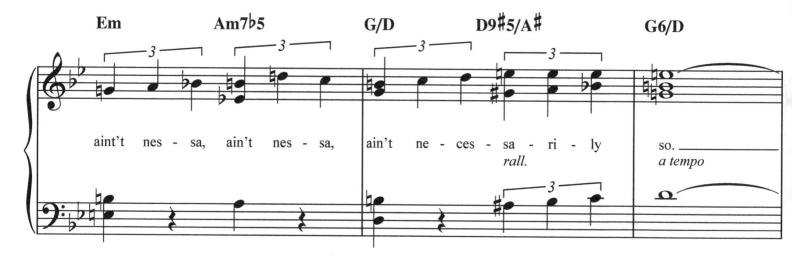

ain't nes - sa, ain't nes - sa, ain't ne - ces - sa - ri - ly so. _____
rall. *a tempo*

LET'S CALL THE WHOLE THING OFF

from SHALL WE DANCE

Music and Lyrics by GEORGE GERSHWIN
and IRA GERSHWIN

Allegretto

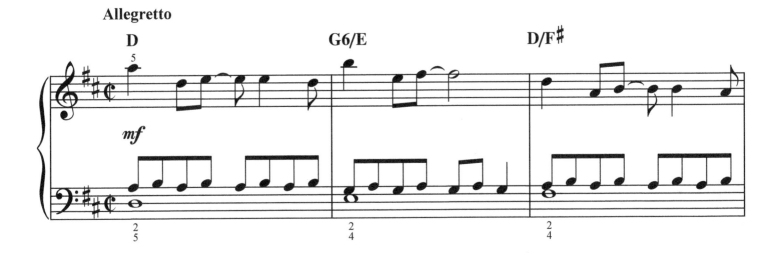

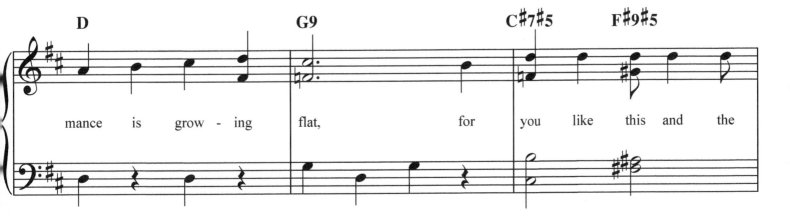

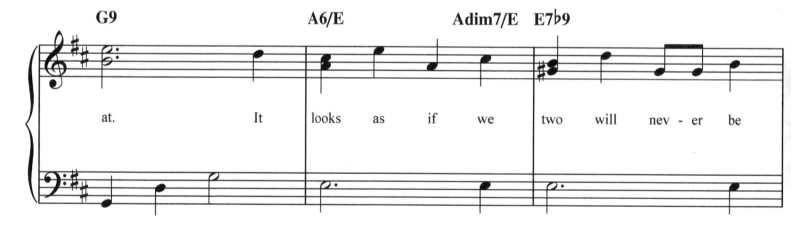

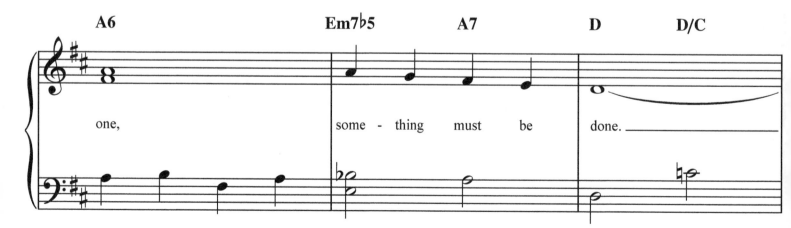

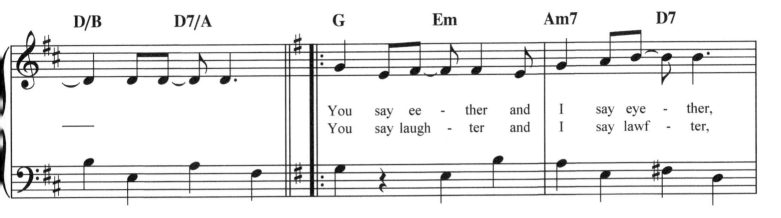

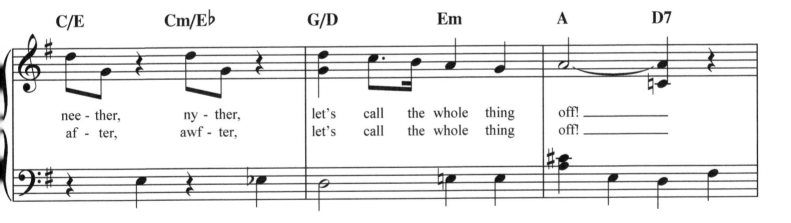

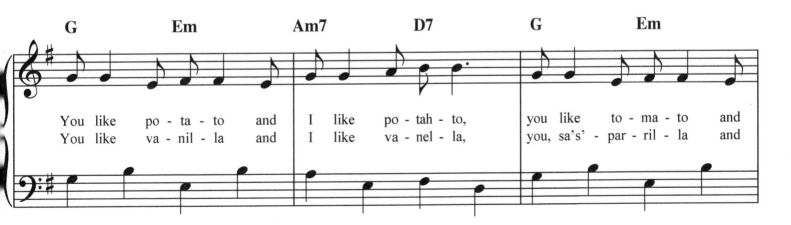

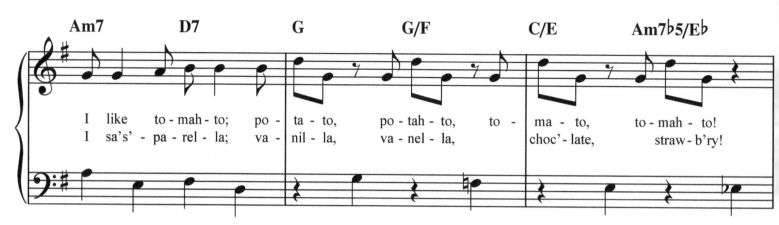

I like to-mah-to; po - ta - to, po - tah - to, to - ma - to, to - mah - to!
I sa's' - pa - rel - la; va - nil - la, va - nel - la, choc' - late, straw - b'ry!

Let's call the whole thing off!
Let's call the whole thing off!
But oh!

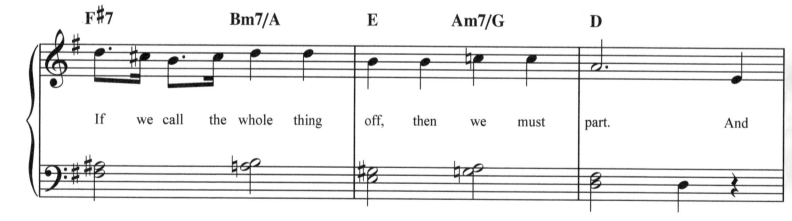

If we call the whole thing off, then we must part. And

oh! If we ev - er part, then that might break my

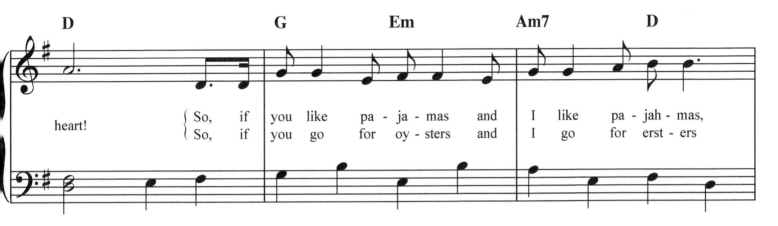

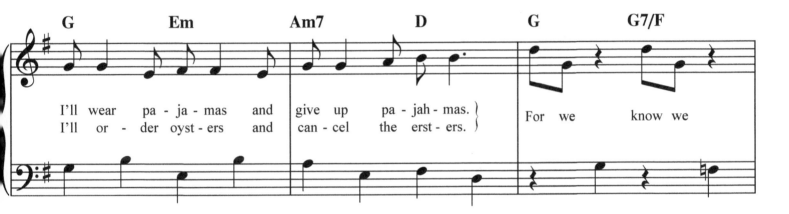

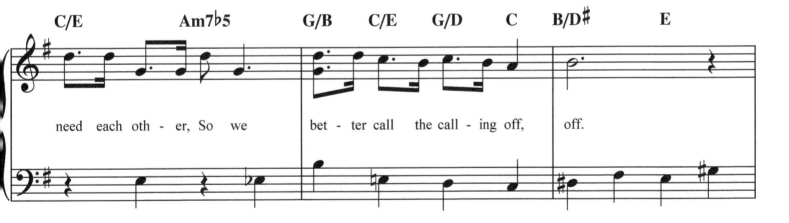

LITTLE JAZZ BIRD

Music and Lyrics by GEORGE GERSHWIN
and IRA GERSHWIN

Moderate Swing

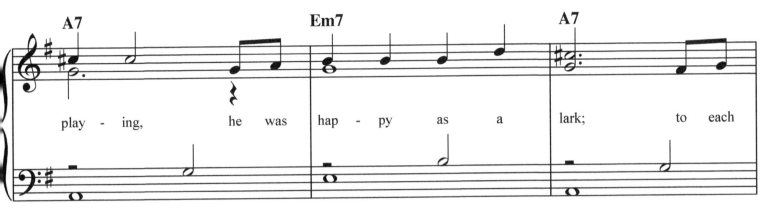

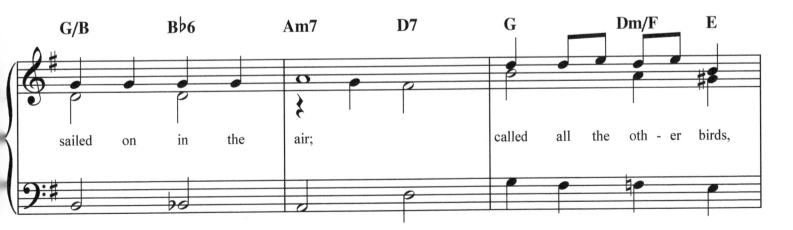

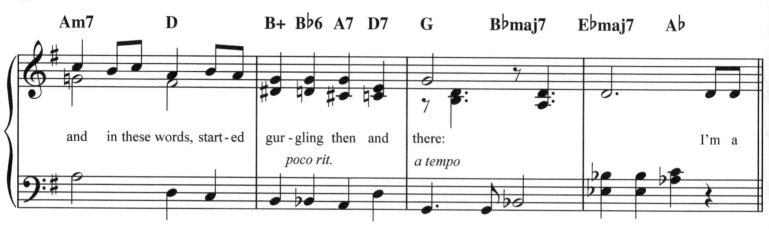

and   in these words, start-ed   gur-gling then and   there: I'm a

poco rit.   *a tempo*

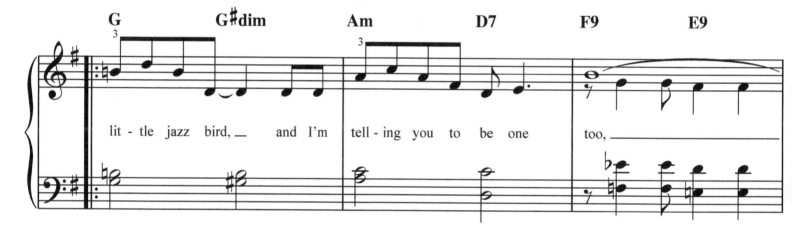

lit - tle jazz bird, __ and I'm   tell - ing you to be one   too, _____

_____ for a   lit - tle jazz bird __ is in   heav - en when it's sing - ing

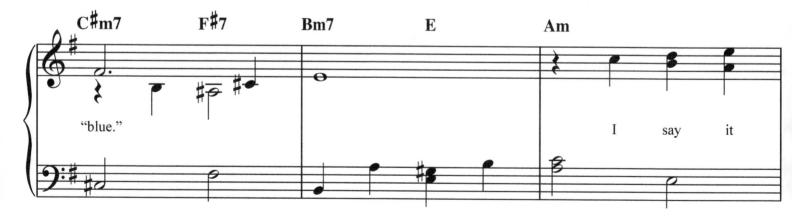

"blue."   I   say   it

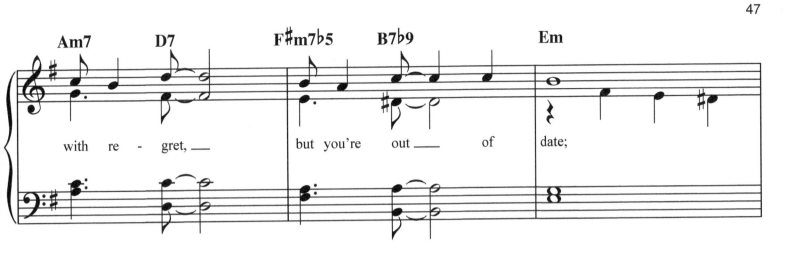

with re - gret, ___ but you're out ___ of date;

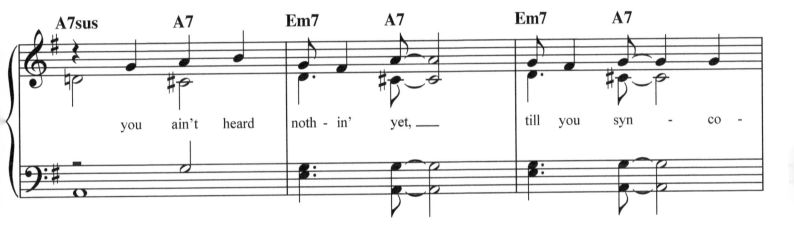

you ain't heard noth - in' yet, ___ till you syn - co -

pate. When the go - ing is rough ___ you will find your trou - bles all have

flown, ___ if you war - ble your stuff ___ like the

moan - ing of a sax - o - phone.

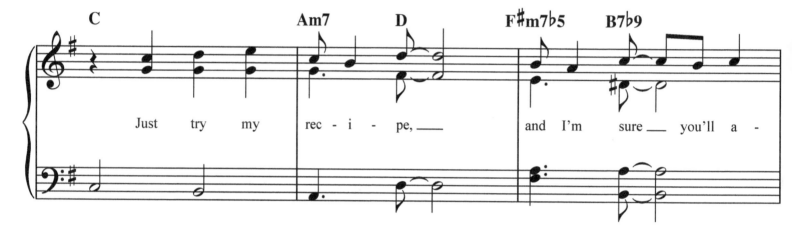

Just try my rec - i - pe, ___ and I'm sure ___ you'll a -

gree that a lit - tle jazz bird ___ is the on - ly kind of bird to

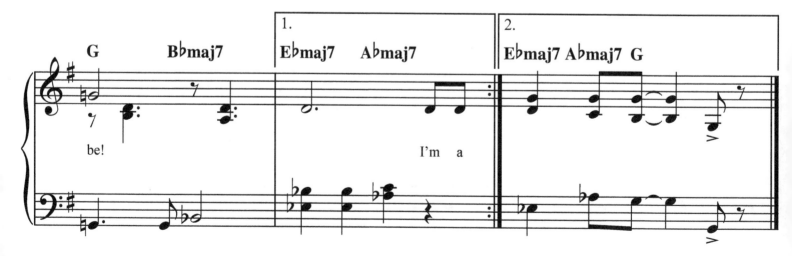

be! I'm a

LOOKING FOR A BOY

Music and Lyrics by GEORGE GERSHWIN
and IRA GERSHWIN

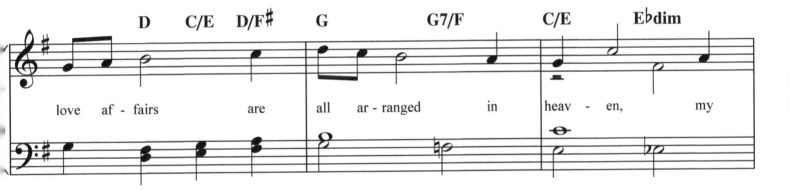

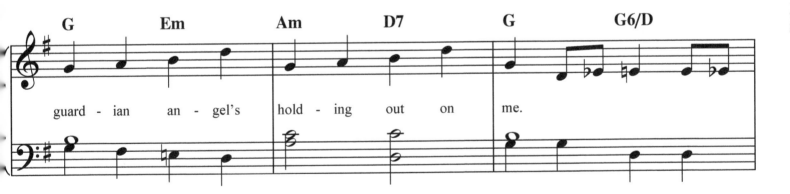

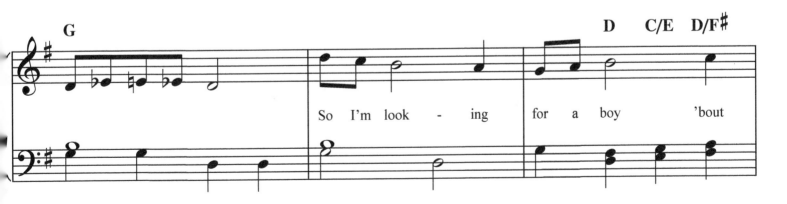

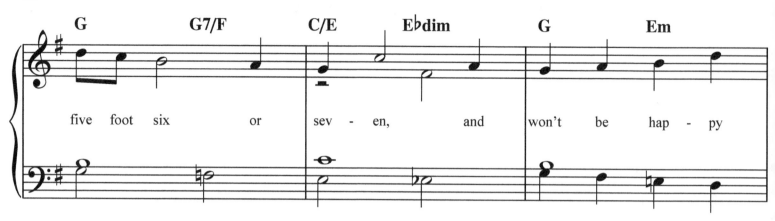

five foot six or sev - en, and won't be hap - py

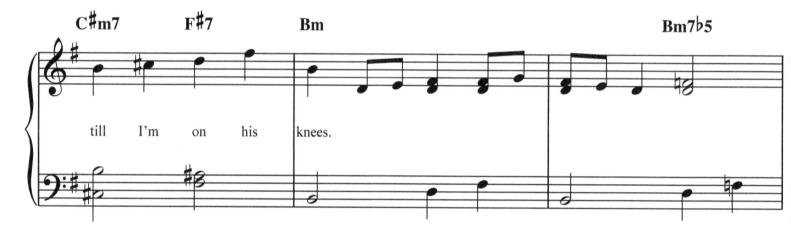

till I'm on his knees.

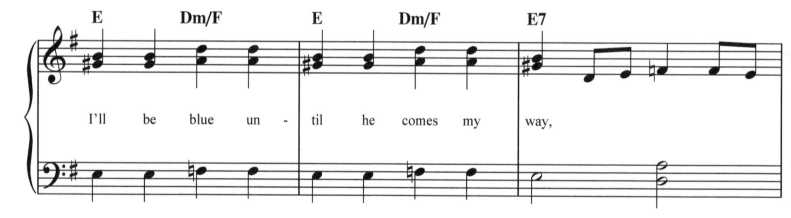

I'll be blue un - til he comes my way,

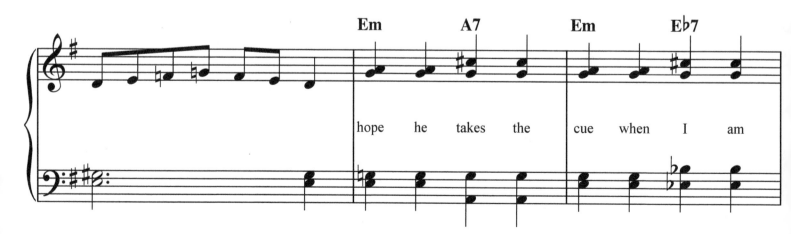

hope he takes the cue when I am

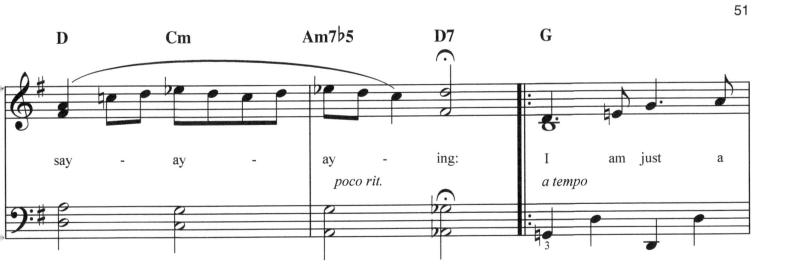

say - ay - ay - ing: I am just a

poco rit.   *a tempo*

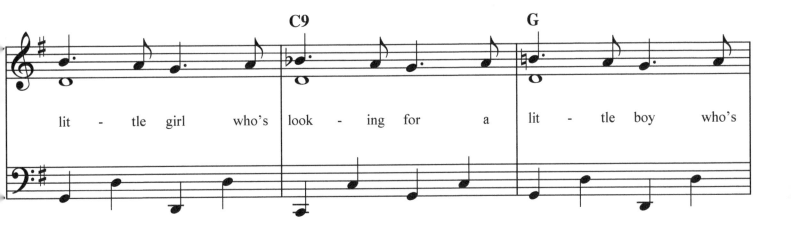

lit - tle girl who's look - ing for a lit - tle boy who's

look - ing for a girl to love.

Tell me, please, where can he be, the

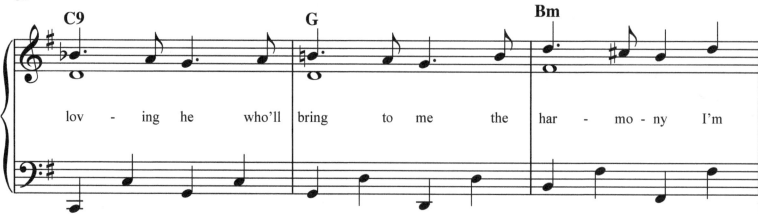

loving he who'll bring to me the har - mo - ny I'm

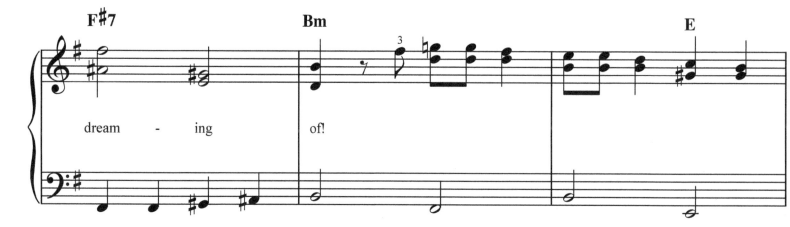

dream - ing of!

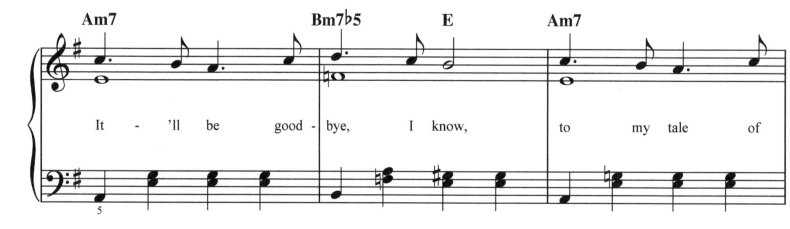

It - 'll be good - bye, I know, to my tale of

woe, when he says, "Hel -

lo!" I am just a

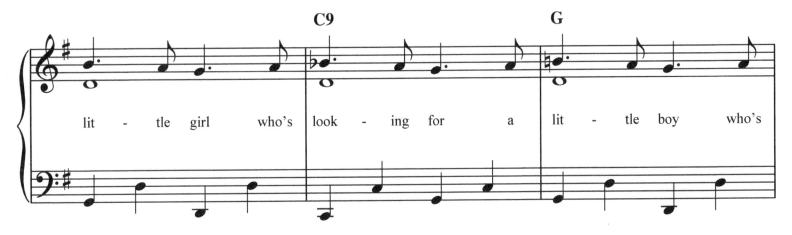

lit - tle girl who's look - ing for a lit - tle boy who's

look - ing for a girl to love.

love.

LIZA
(All the Clouds'll Roll Away)

Music by GEORGE GERSHWIN
Lyrics by IRA GERSHWIN and GUS KAHN

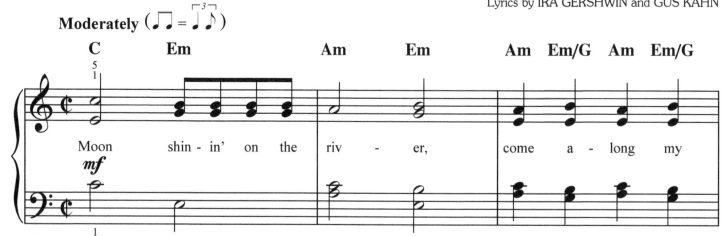

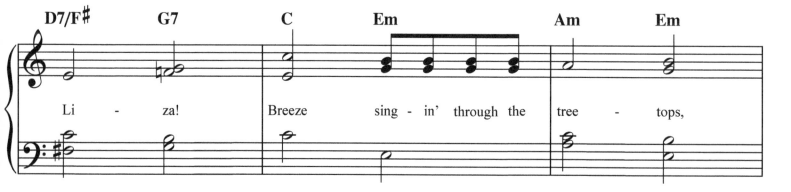

I get lone-some, hon-ey, when I'm all a-lone so long. Don't make me wait;

don't hes - i - tate; come and hear my song.

Li - za, Li - za, skies are
Li - za, Li - za, don't de -

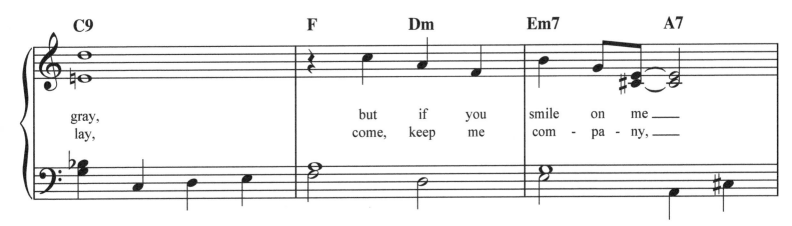

gray, but if you smile on me
lay, come, keep me com - pa - ny,

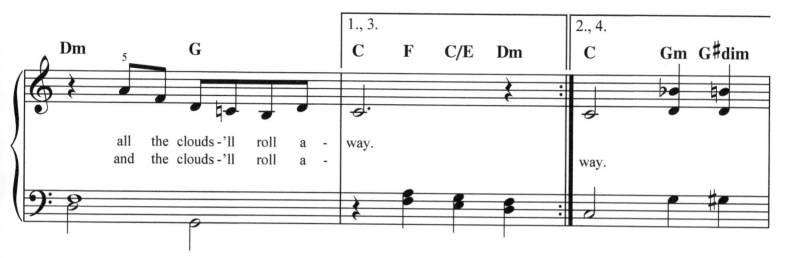

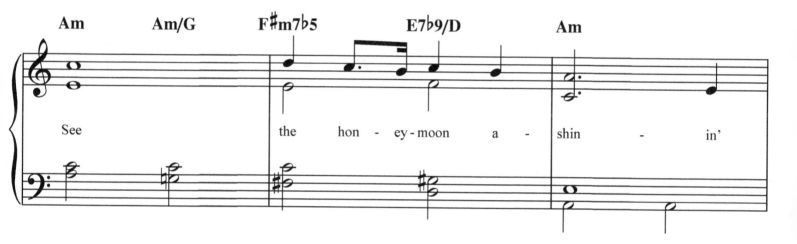

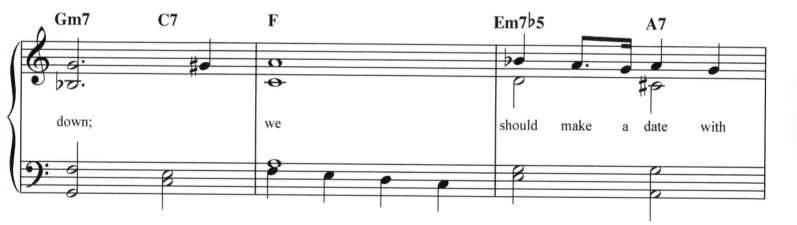

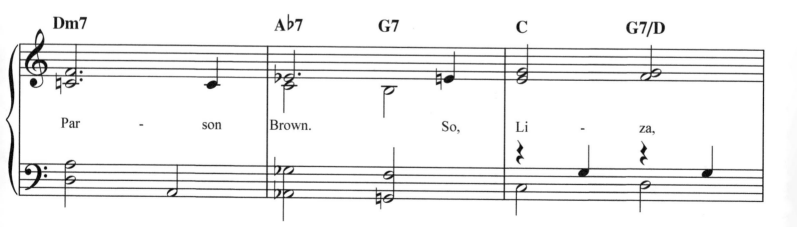

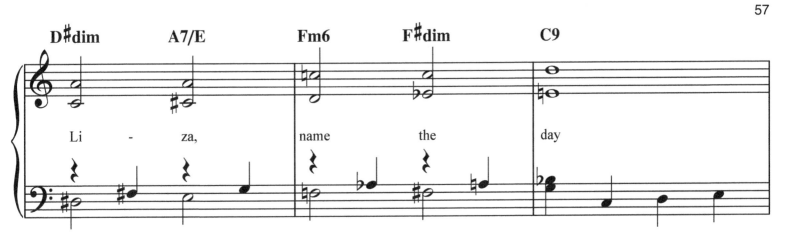

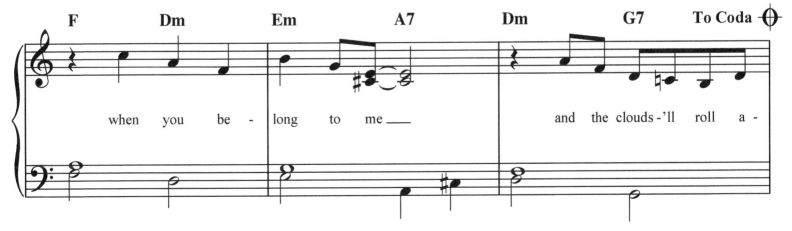

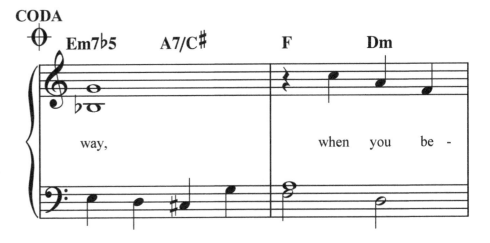

LOVE IS HERE TO STAY

from GOLDWYN FOLLIES

Music and Lyrics by GEORGE GERSHWIN
and IRA GERSHWIN

With motion

The more I read the pa - pers the less I com - pre -

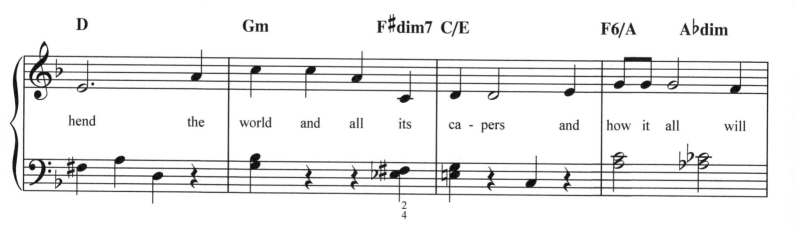

hend the world and all its ca - pers and how it all will

end. Noth - ing seems to be last - ing, but

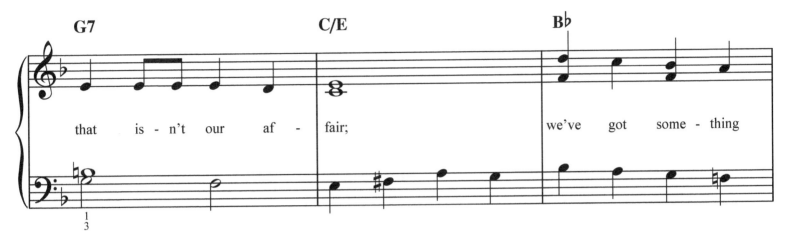

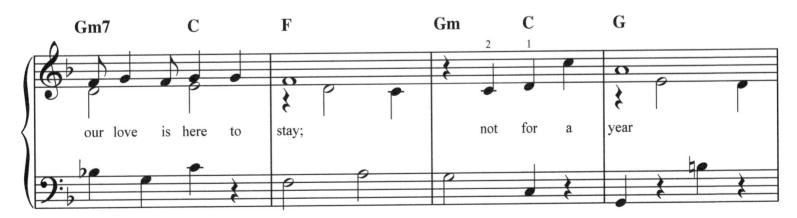

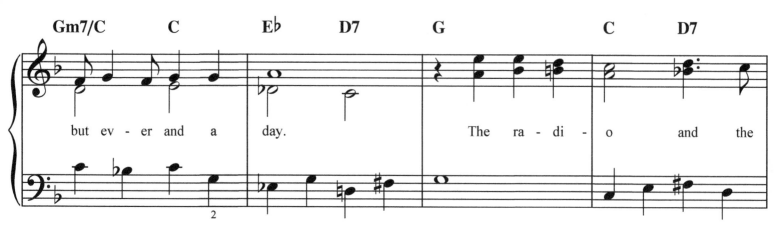

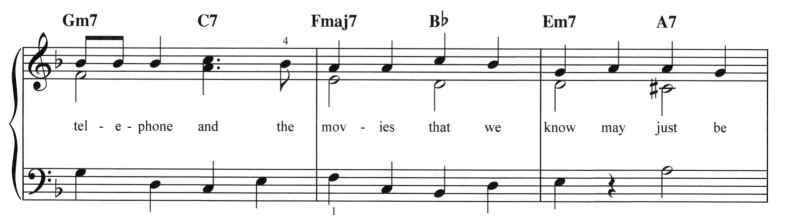

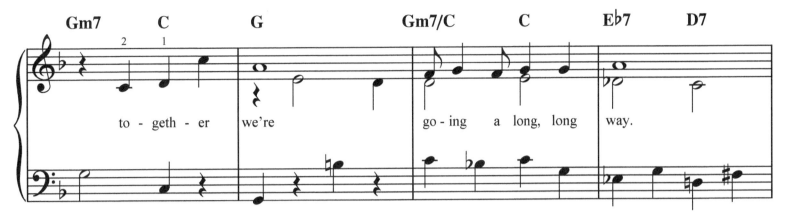

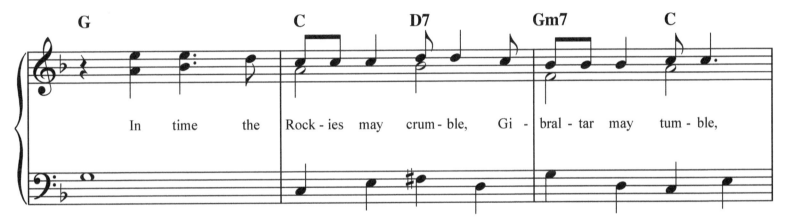

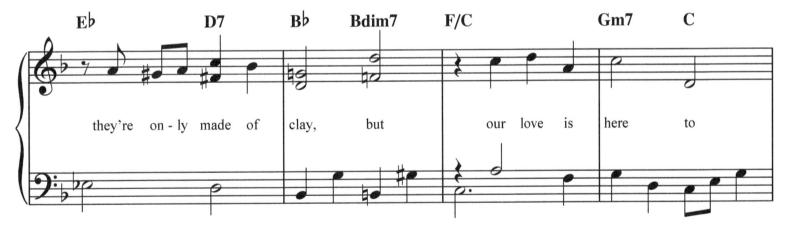

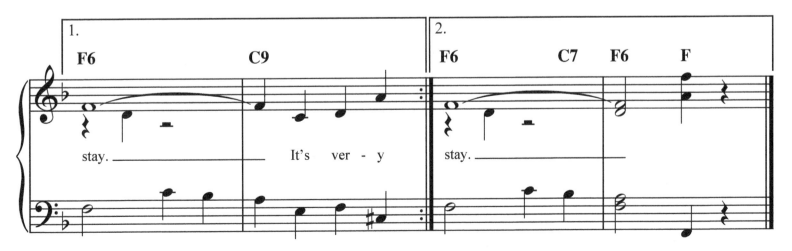

LOVED WALKED IN

Music and Lyrics by GEORGE GERSHWIN
and IRA GERSHWIN

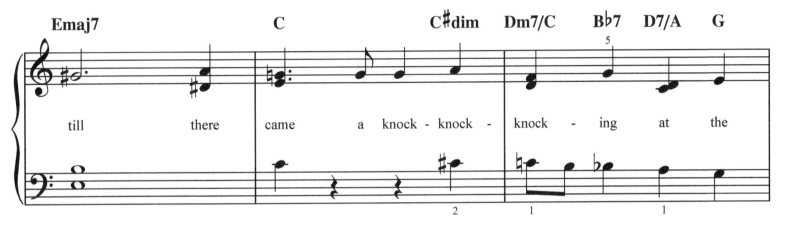

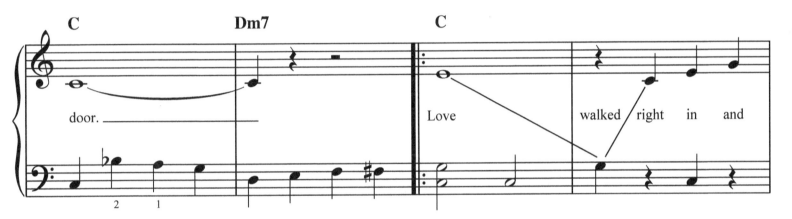

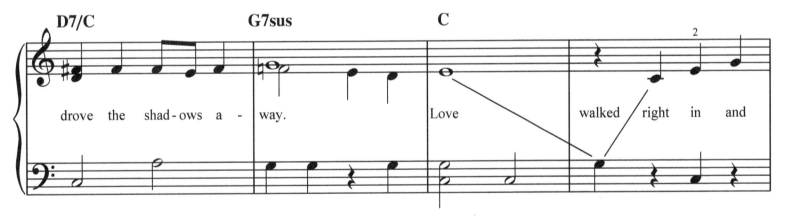

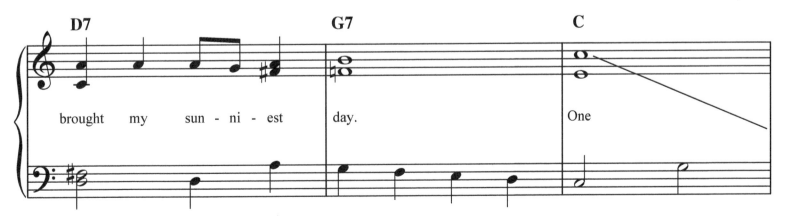

64

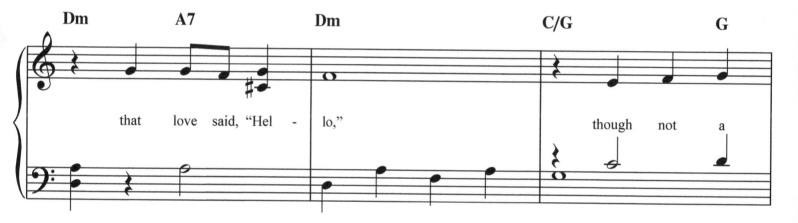

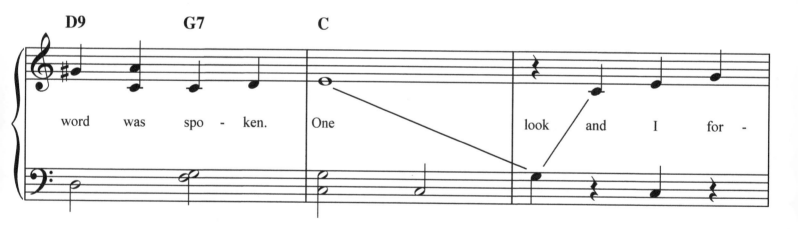

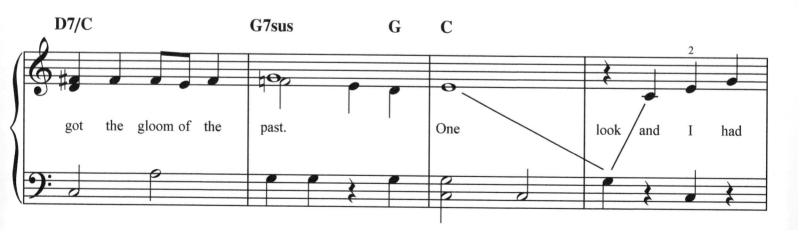

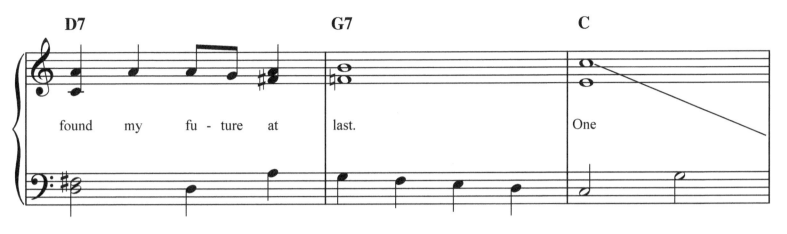

found my fu - ture at   last.   One

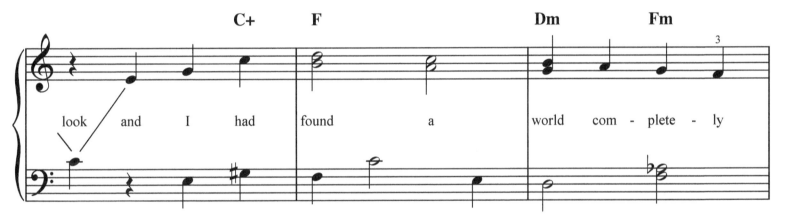

look   and   I   had   found   a   world com - plete - ly

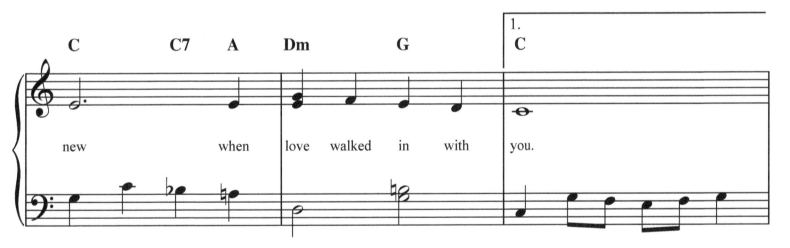

new   when   love   walked   in   with   you.

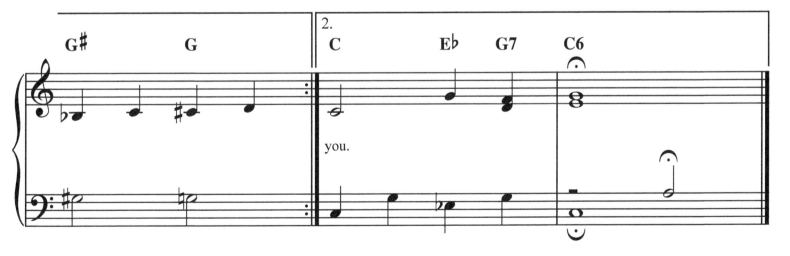

you.

MAYBE

Music and Lyrics by GEORGE GERSHWIN
and IRA GERSHWIN

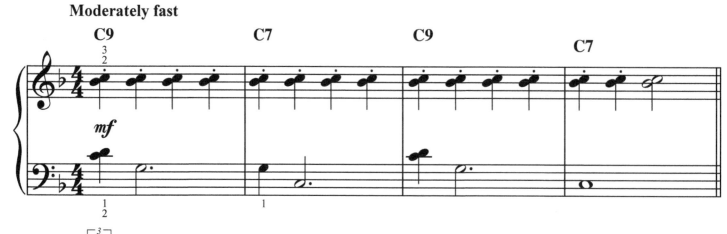

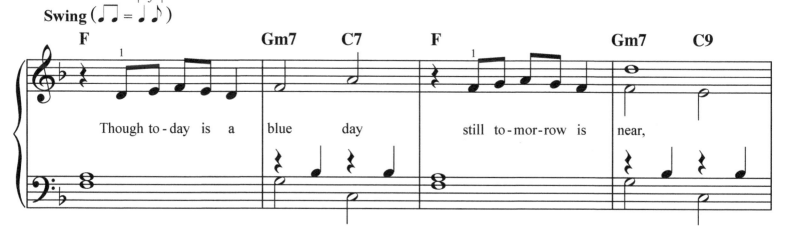

Though to-day is a blue day still to-mor-row is near,

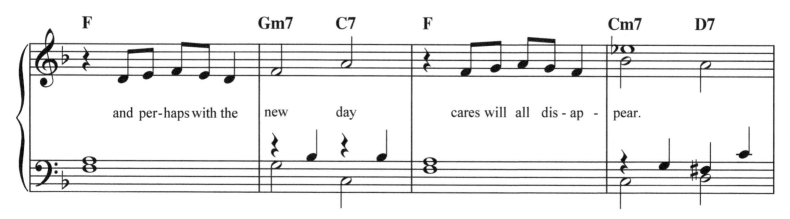

and per-haps with the new day cares will all dis-ap - pear.

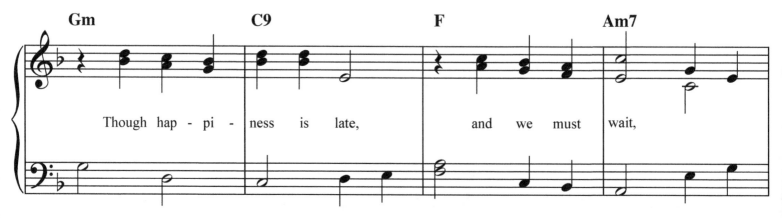

Though hap-pi - ness is late, and we must wait,

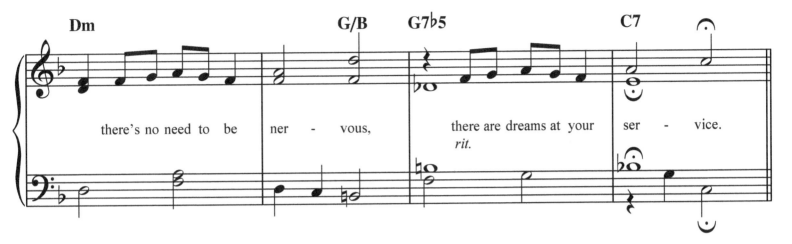

there's no need to be ner - vous,   there are dreams at your ser - vice.
rit.

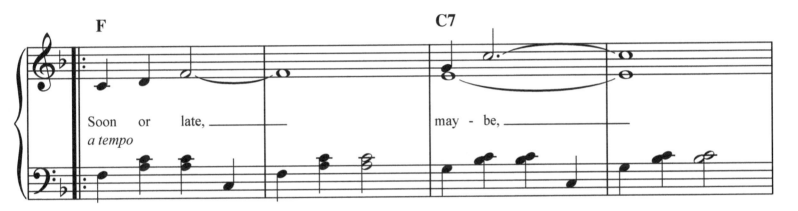

Soon or late, _____   may - be, _____
a tempo

if you wait, _____   may - be, _____

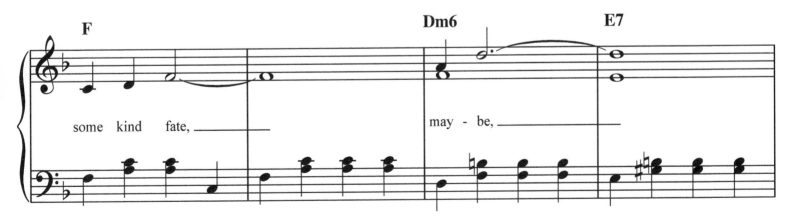

some kind fate, _____   may - be, _____

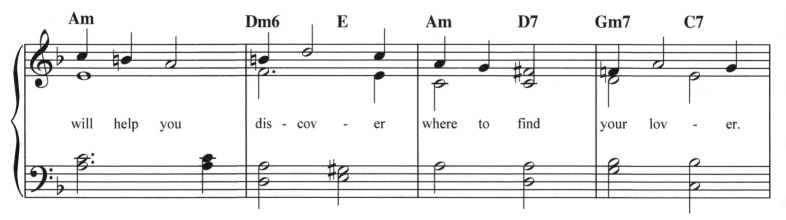

will help you dis - cov - er where to find your lov - er.

will you hear you - hoo,

he'll be near ___ you - hoo.

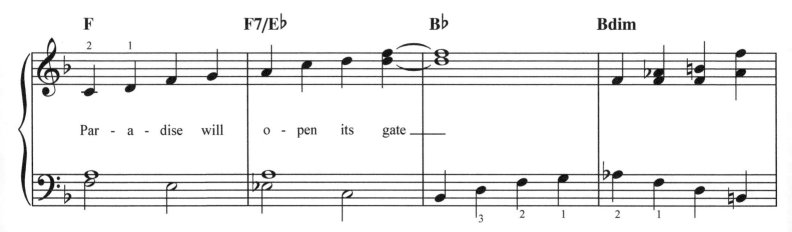

Par - a - dise will o - pen its gate ___

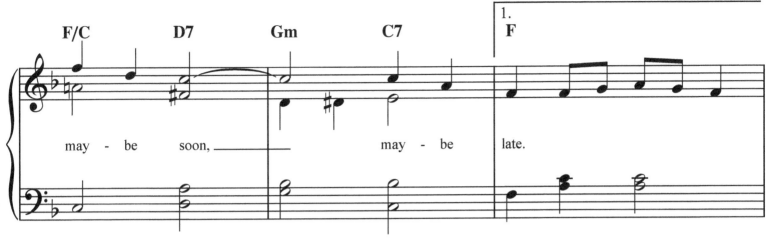

may - be soon, _____ may - be late.

late.

May - be soon, _____

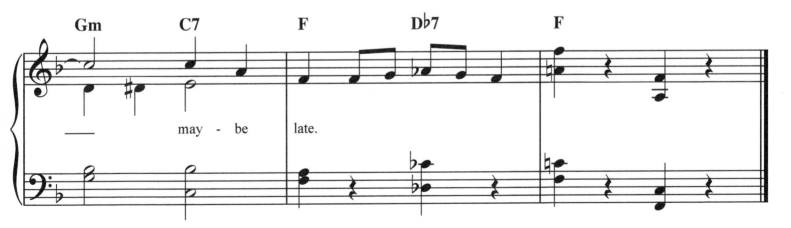

may - be late.

'S WONDERFUL
from FUNNY FACE

Music and Lyrics by GEORGE GERSHWIN
and IRA GERSHWIN

Moderately slow, rubato

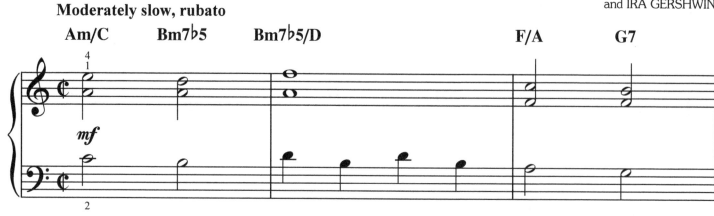

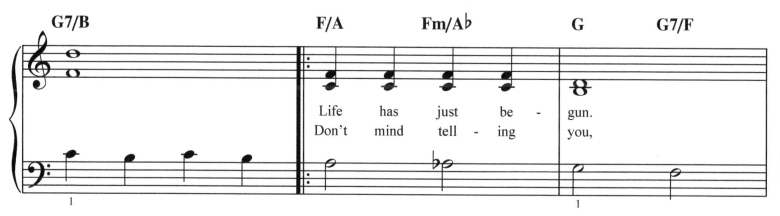

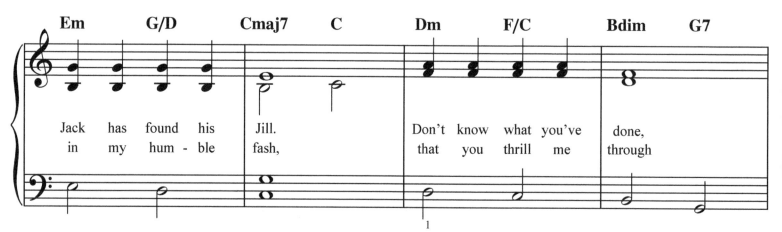

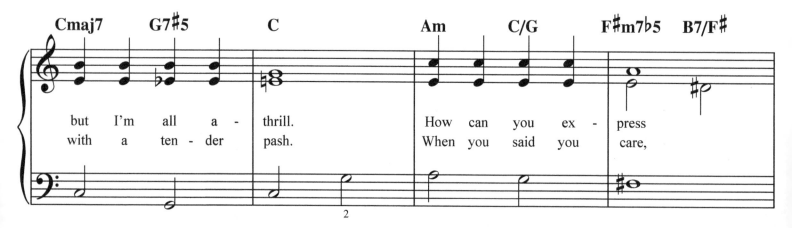

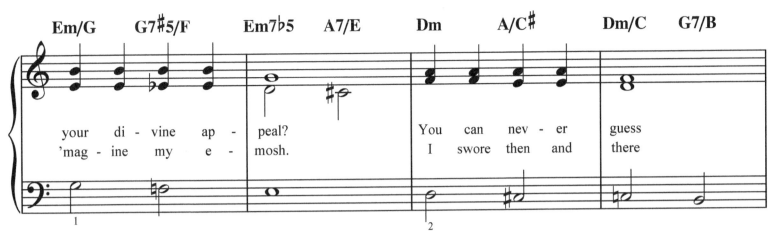

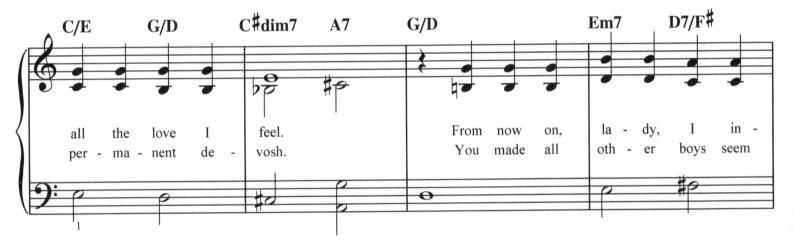

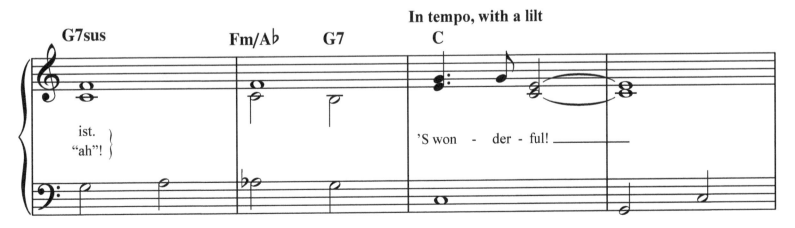

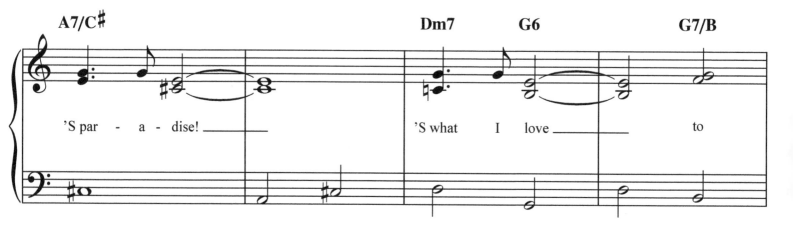

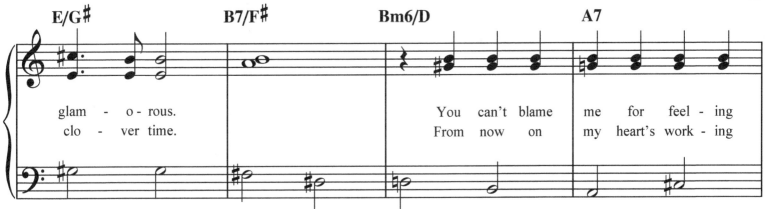

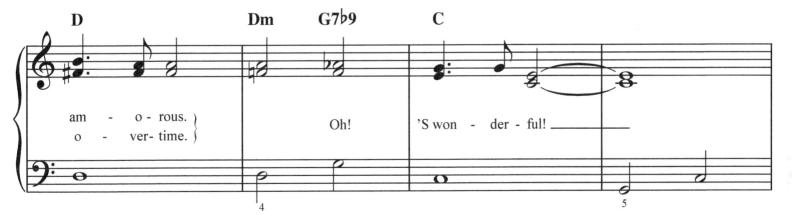

SOMEBODY LOVES ME
from GEORGE WHITE'S SCANDALS OF 1924

Music by GEORGE GERSHWIN
Lyrics by B.G. DeSYLVA and BALLARD MacDONALD
French Version by EMELIA RENAUD

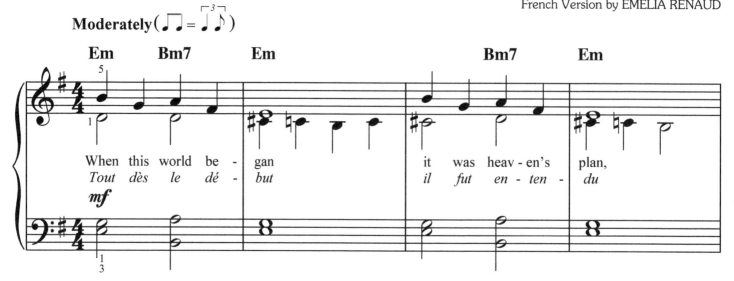

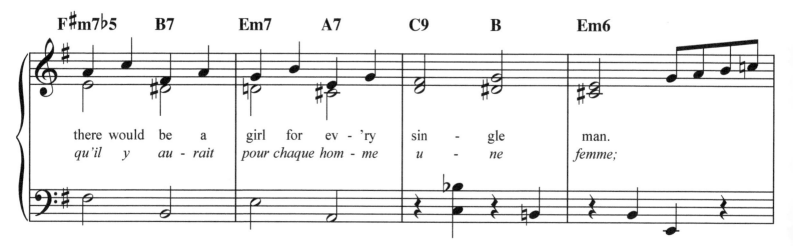

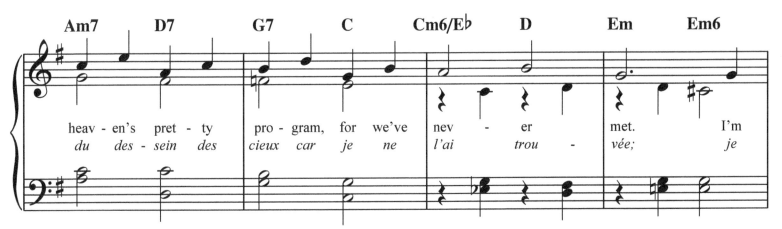

heav - en's pret - ty pro - gram, for we've nev - er met. I'm
du des - sein des cieux car je ne l'ai trou - vée; je

clutch - ing at straws, just be - cause I may meet her yet.
veux es - pé - rer qu'un jour je la ren - con - tre - rai.
rit.

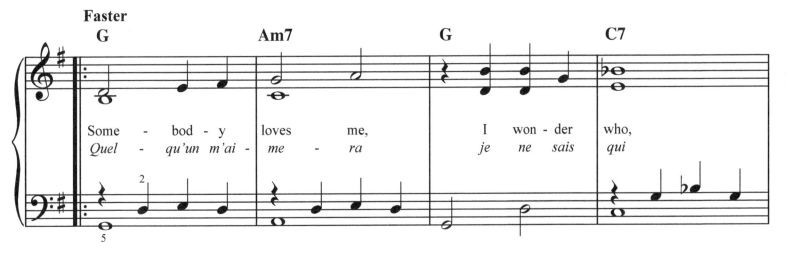

Faster

Some - bod - y loves me, I won - der who,
Quel - qu'un m'ai - me - ra je ne sais qui

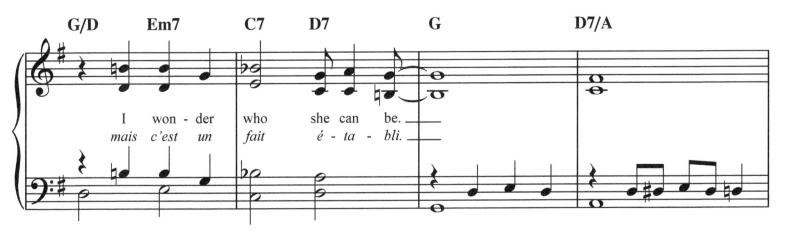

I won - der who she can be.
mais c'est un fait é - ta - bli.

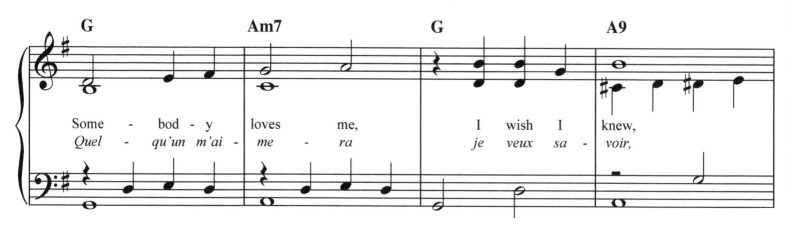

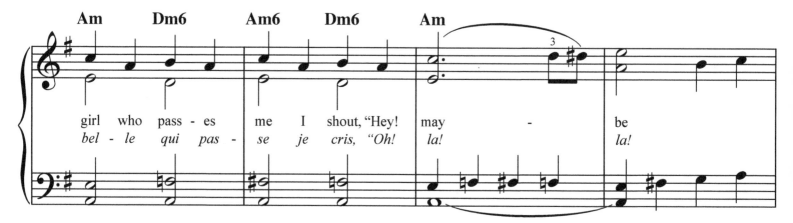

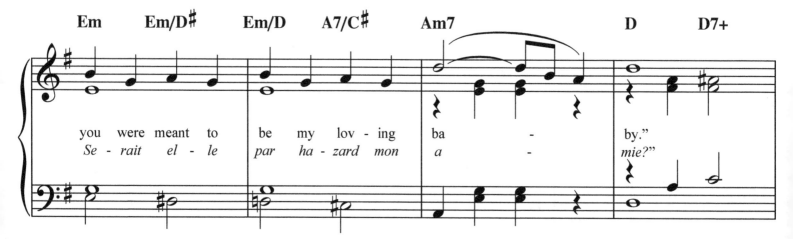

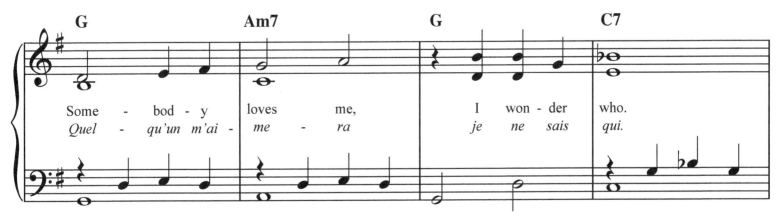

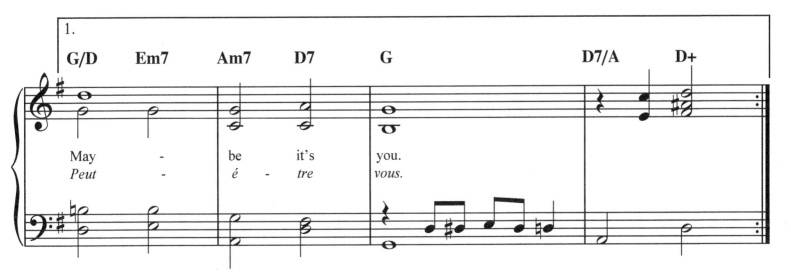

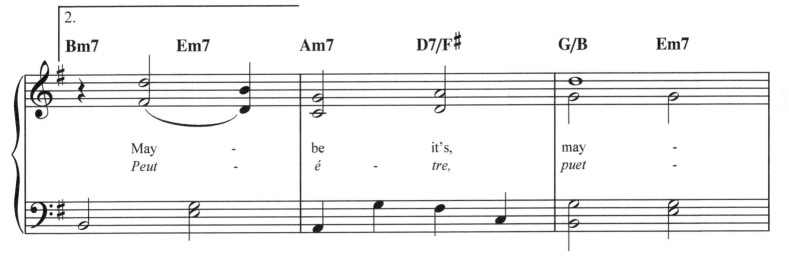

SOON
from STRIKE UP THE BAND

Music and Lyrics by GEORGE GERSHWIN
and IRA GERSHWIN

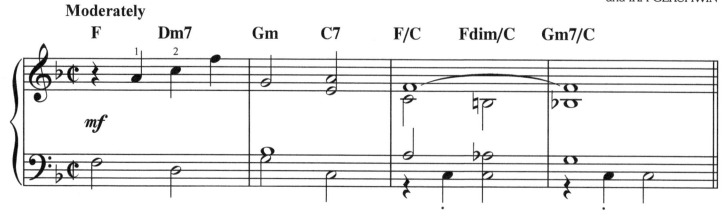

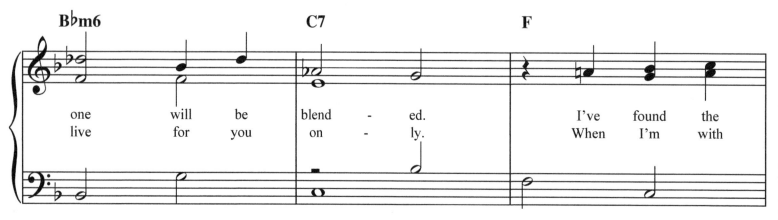

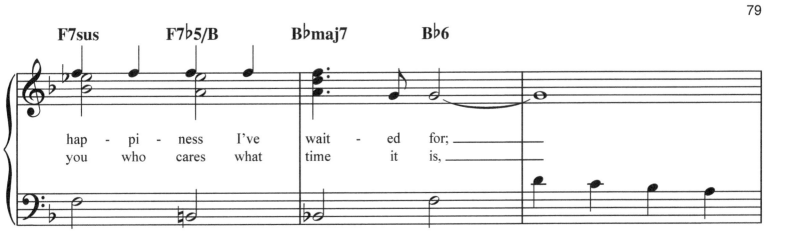

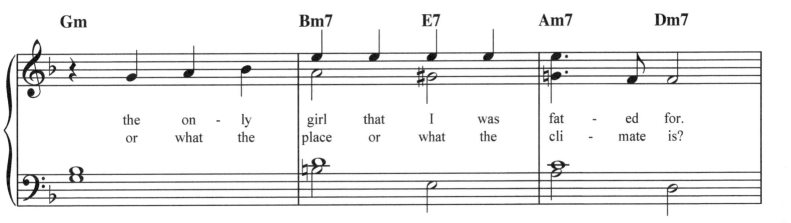

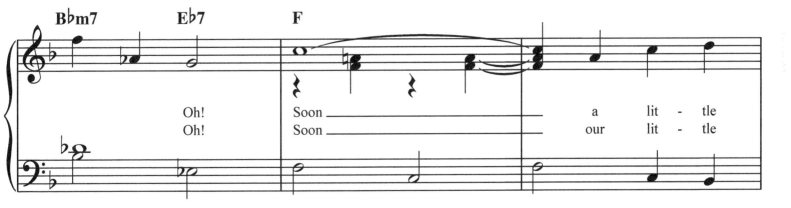

cares   far   be - hind   us.
storm,   nev - er   fail - ing.   The   day   you're

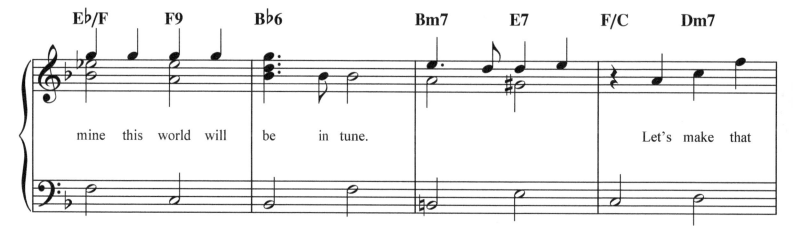

mine   this   world   will   be   in   tune.   Let's   make   that

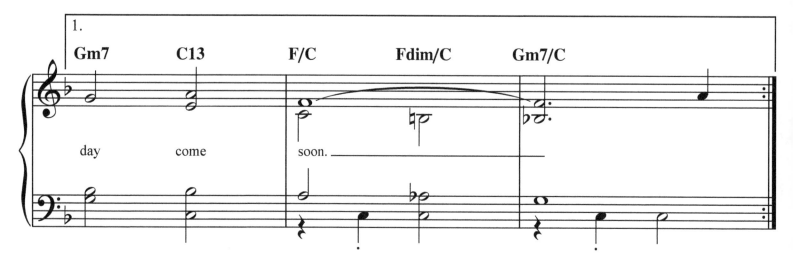

day   come   soon. _____

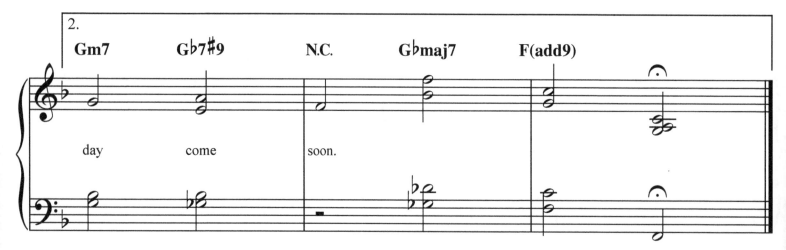

day   come   soon.

SOMEONE TO WATCH OVER ME

from OH, KAY!

Music and Lyrics by GEORGE GERSHWIN
and IRA GERSHWIN

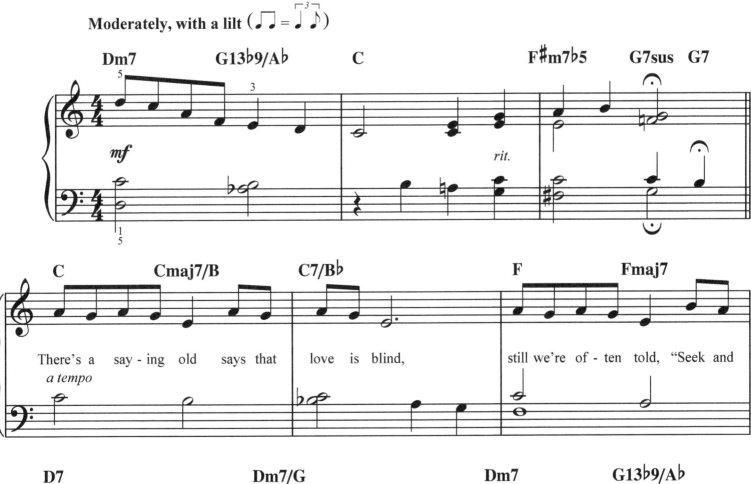

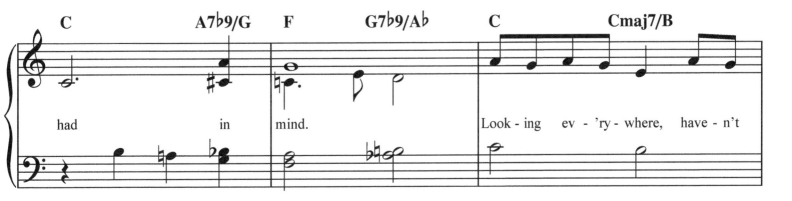

82

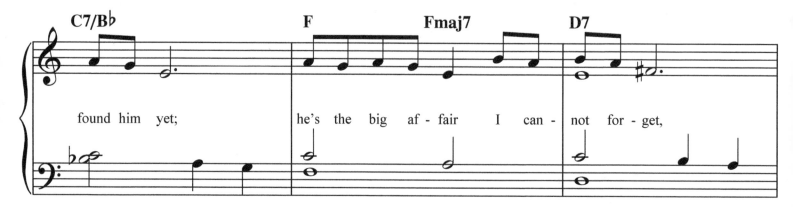

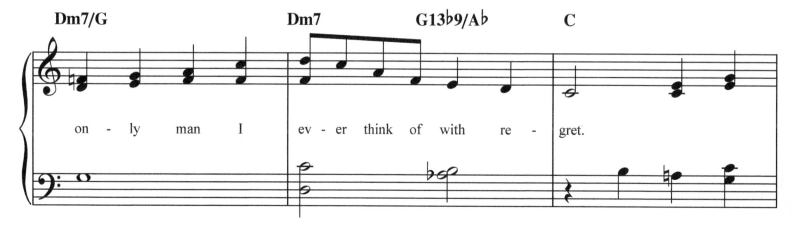

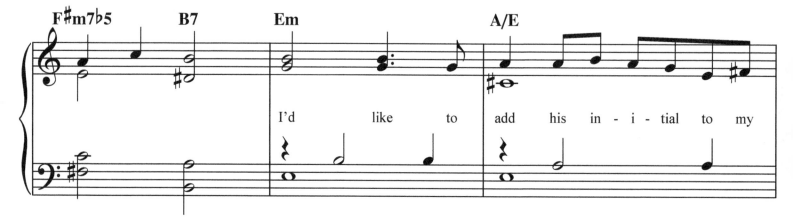

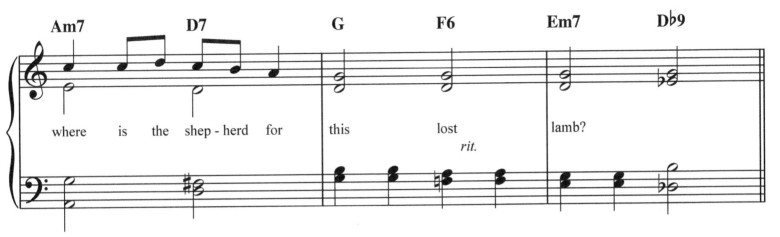

where is the shep - herd for this lost lamb?

rit.

There's a some - bod - y I'm long - ing to see. I hope that he

a tempo

turns out to be some - one who'll watch o - ver

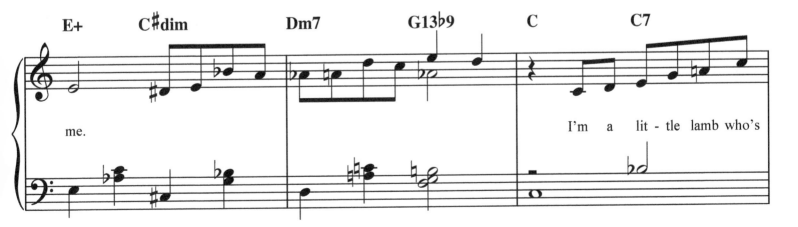

me. I'm a lit - tle lamb who's

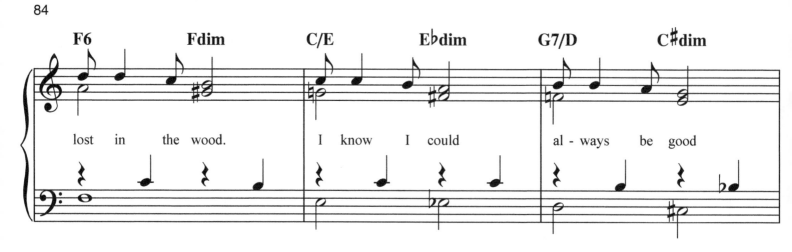

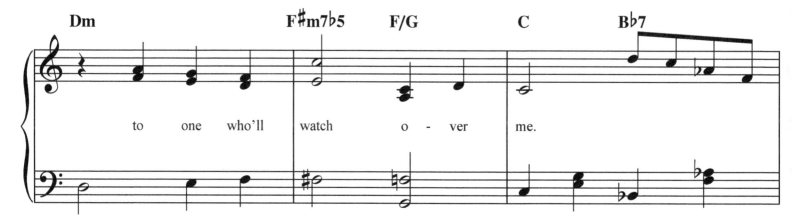

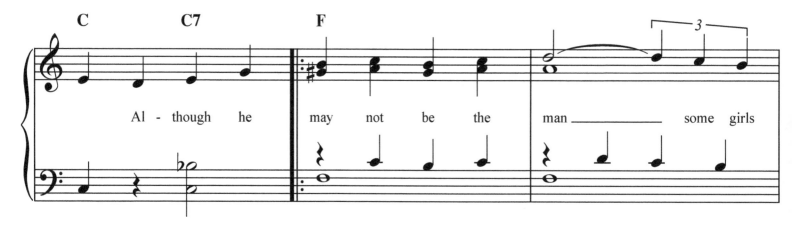

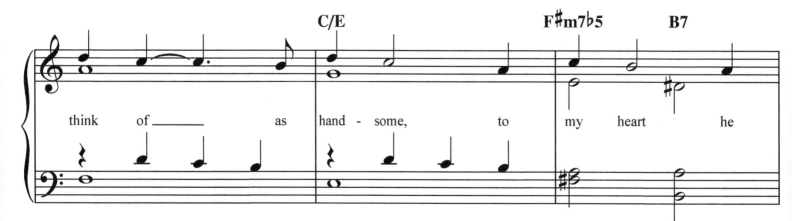

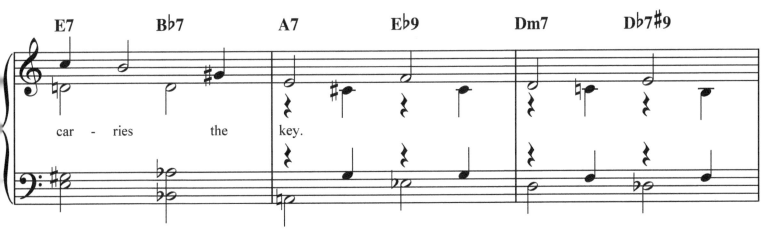

car - ries the key.

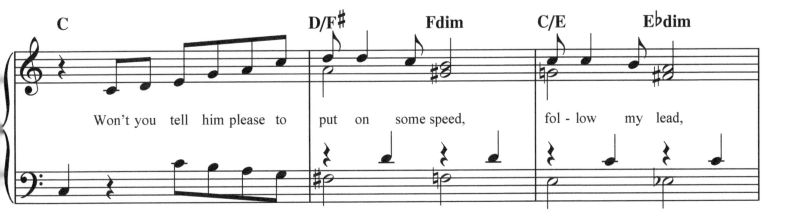

Won't you tell him please to put on some speed, fol - low my lead,

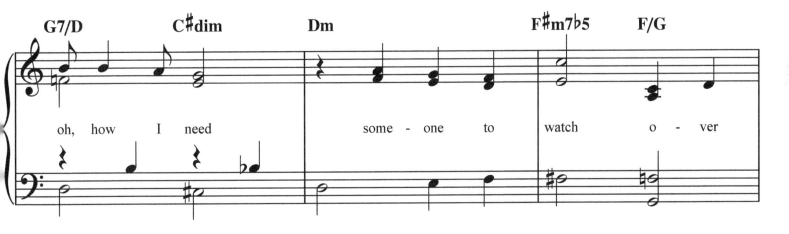

oh, how I need some - one to watch o - ver

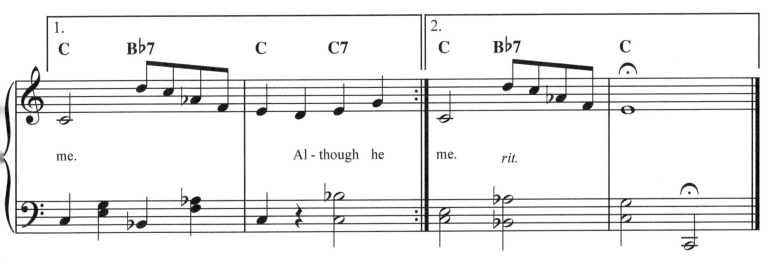

me.   Al - though he   me. *rit.*

SUMMERTIME
from PORGY AND BESS ®

Words and Music by GEORGE GERSHWIN,
DuBOSE and DOROTHY HEYWARD
and IRA GERSHWIN

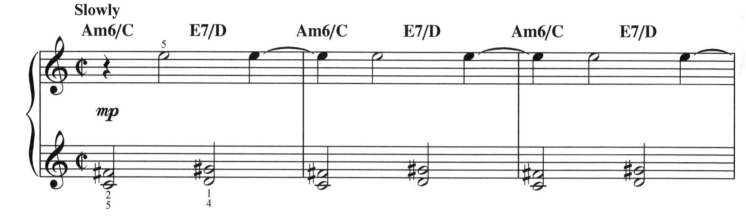

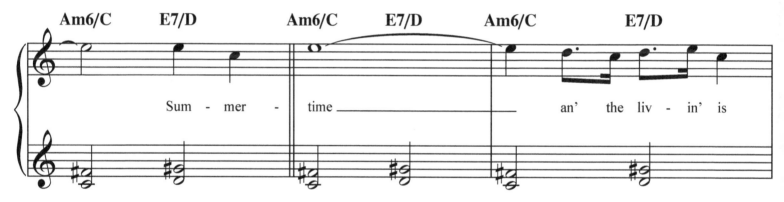

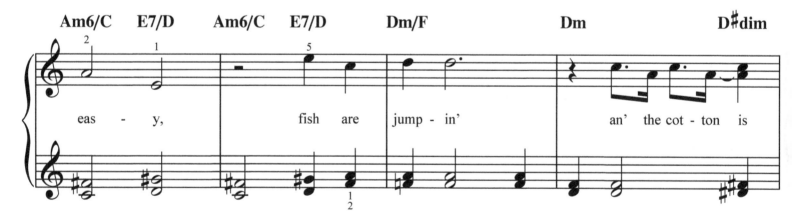

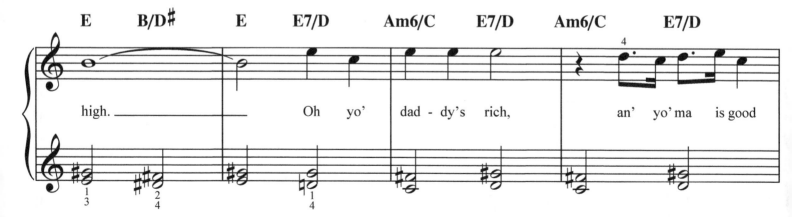

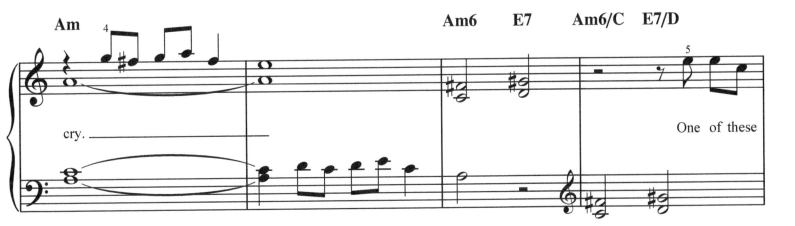

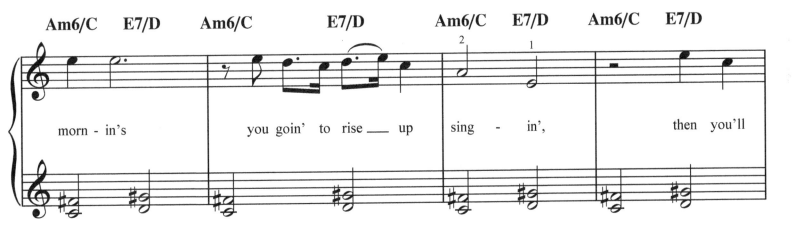

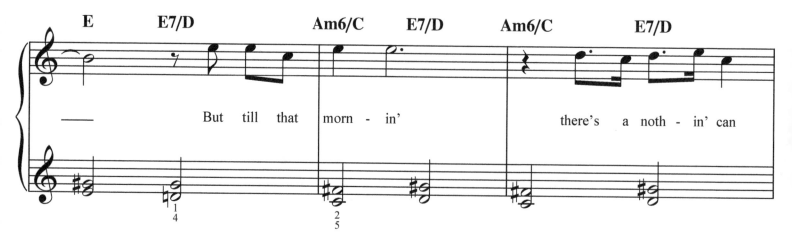

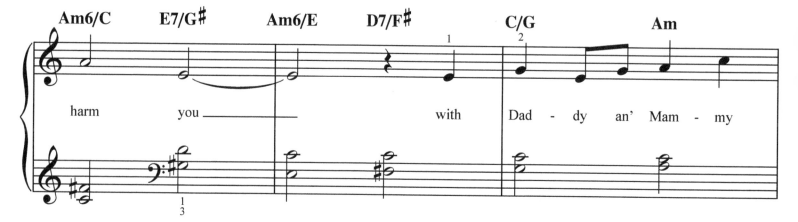

THEY ALL LAUGHED

Music and Lyrics by GEORGE GERSHWIN
and IRA GERSHWIN

Simply, freely

The odds were a hun - dred to one a -

gainst me. The world thought the

heights were too high to climb. But

peo - ple from Mis - sou - ri nev - er in - censed me.

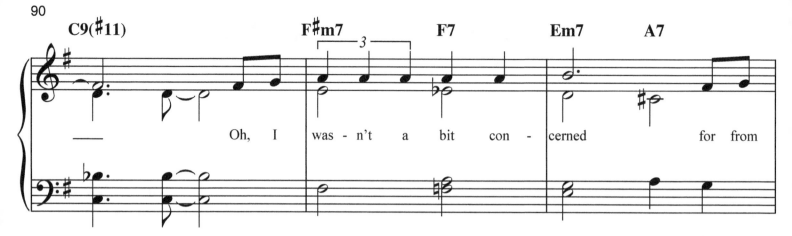

C9(#11)   **F#m7**   **F7**   **Em7**   **A7**

Oh, I was-n't a bit con - cerned for from

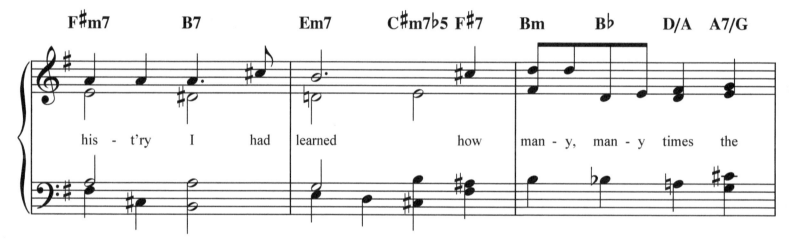

F#m7   **B7**   **Em7**   **C#m7♭5 F#7**   **Bm**   **B♭**   **D/A A7/G**

his - t'ry I had learned how man - y, man - y times the

D/F#   **Em7 A7/E Am7/D**   **D**

worm had turned.   *rit.*   *mf*

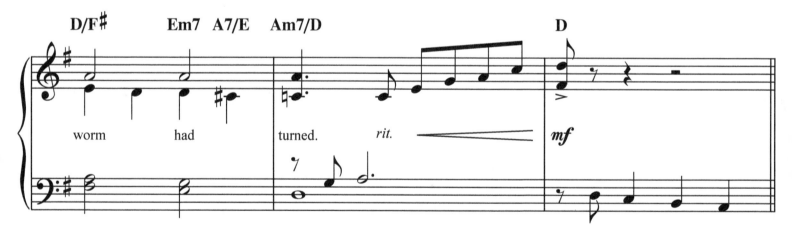

Moderate Swing (♩♩ = 𝅘𝅥𝅮³𝅘𝅥𝅮)

G   **Em**   **Am7**   **D7**   **Am7**   **D7**

They all laughed at Chris-to-pher Co-lum-bus when he said the world was round.
They all laughed at Rock-e-fel-ler Cen-ter; now they're fight-ing to get in.

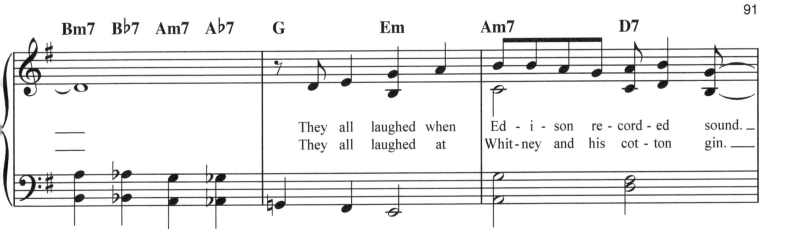

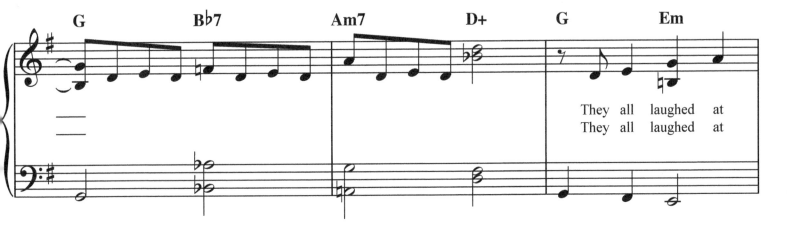

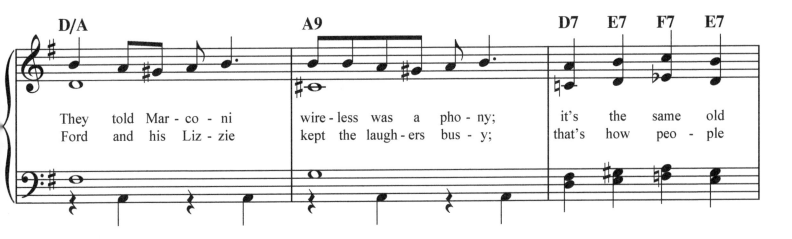

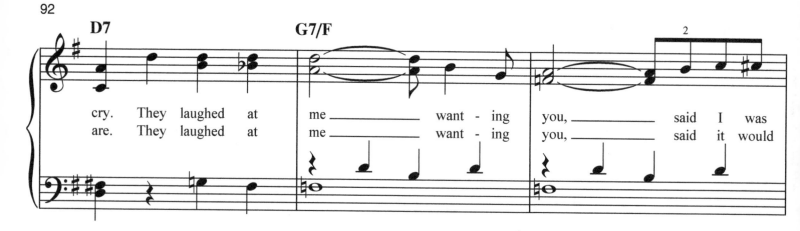

cry. They laughed at me _____ want - ing you, _____ said I was
are. They laughed at me _____ want - ing you, _____ said it would

reach - ing for the moon; but oh, _____ you came
be hel - lo good - bye; but oh, _____ you came

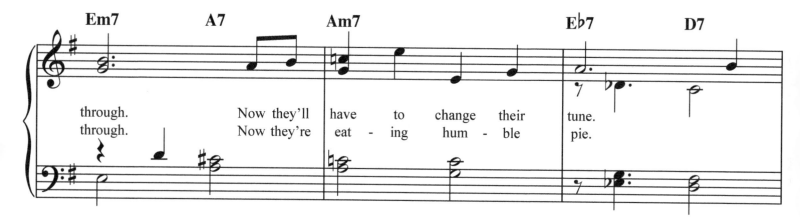

through. Now they'll have to change their tune.
through. Now they're eat - ing hum - ble pie.

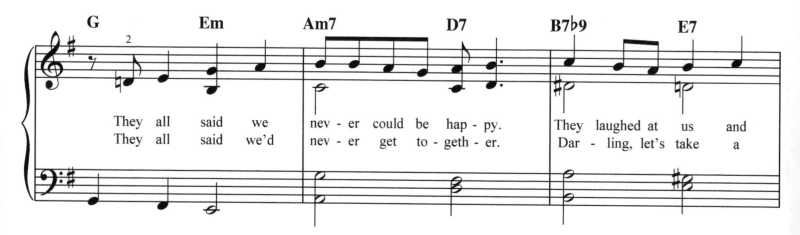

They all said we nev - er could be hap - py. They laughed at us and
They all said we'd nev - er get to - geth - er. Dar - ling, let's take a

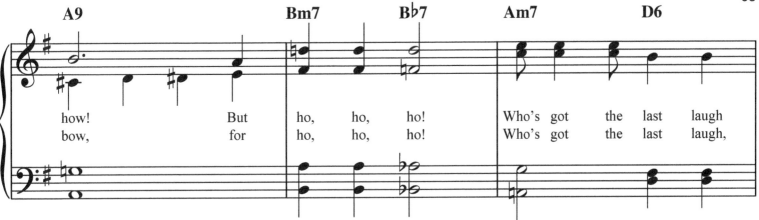

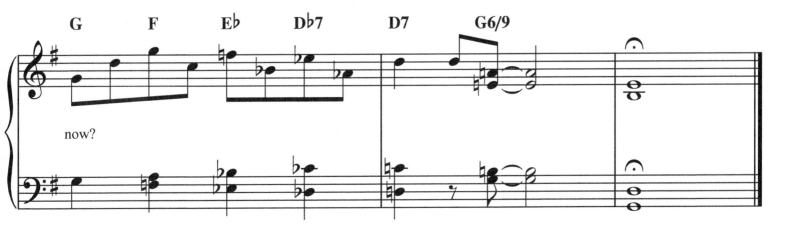

WHO CARES?
(So Long as You Care for Me)
from OF THEE I SING

Music and Lyrics by GEORGE GERSHWIN
and IRA GERSHWIN

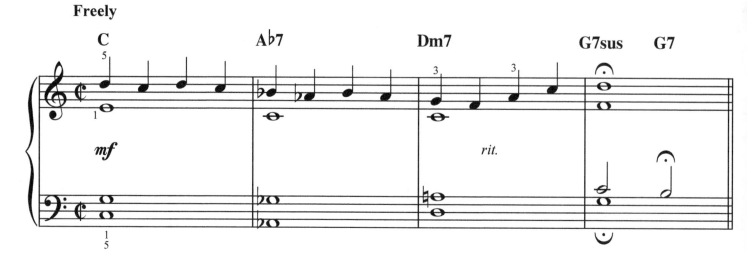

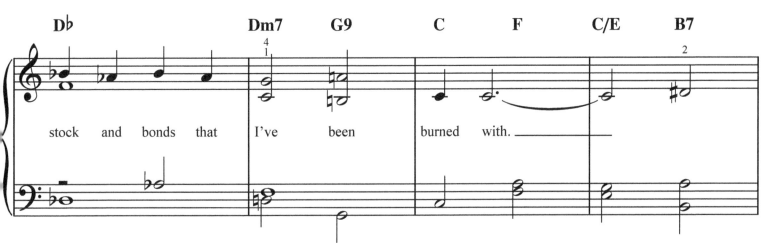

stock and bonds that I've been burned with. _____

I love you and you love me. And that's how it will

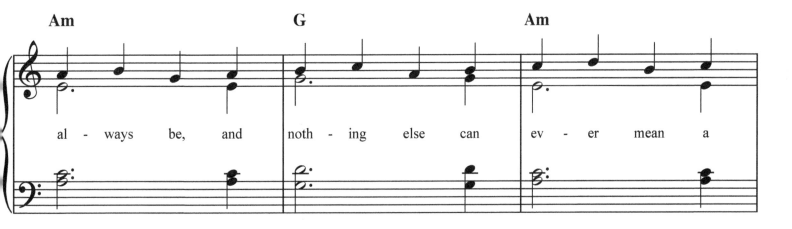

al - ways be, and noth - ing else can ev - er mean a

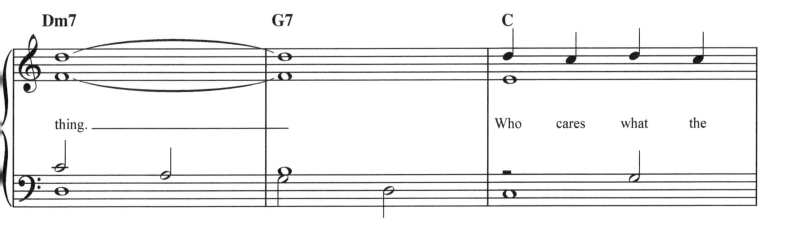

thing. _____ Who cares what the

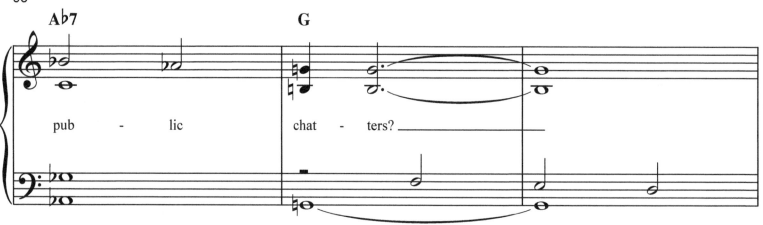

pub - lic   chat - ters? _____

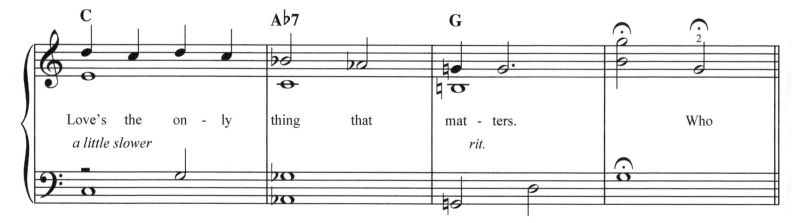

Love's the on - ly   thing that   mat - ters.   Who
a little slower   *rit.*

Brightly

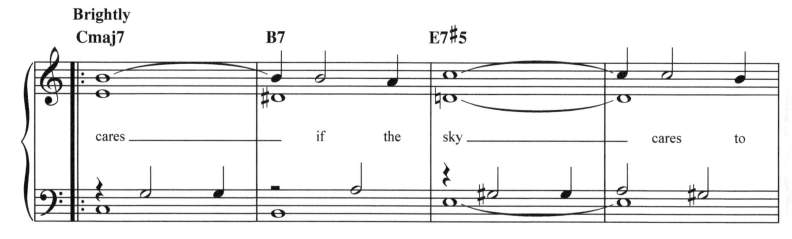

cares _____ if the sky _____ cares to

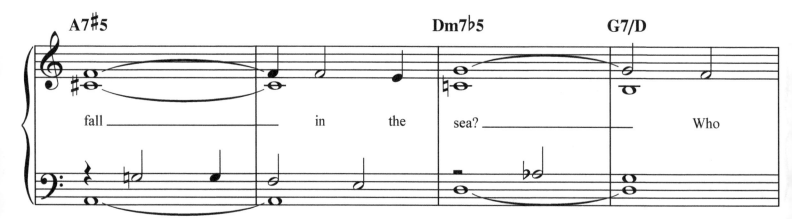

fall _____ in the sea? _____ Who

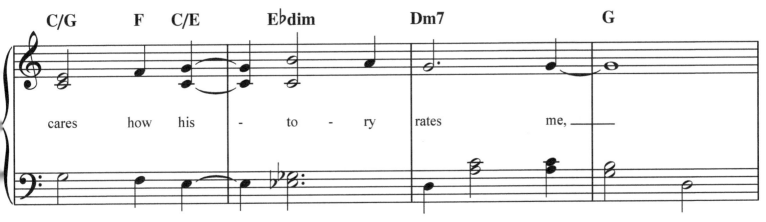

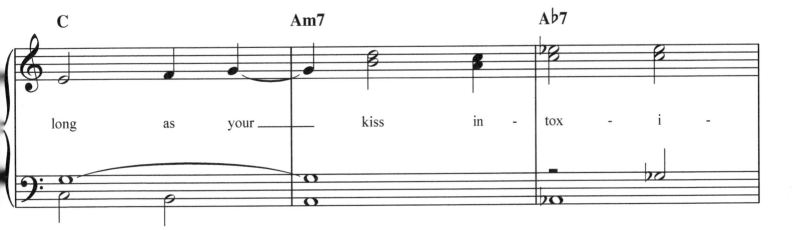

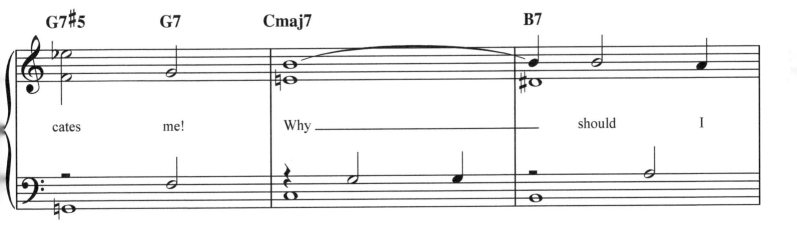

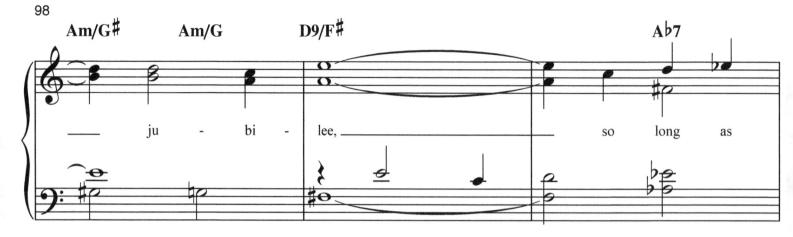

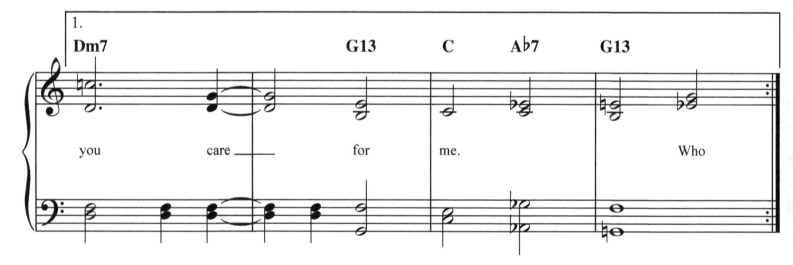

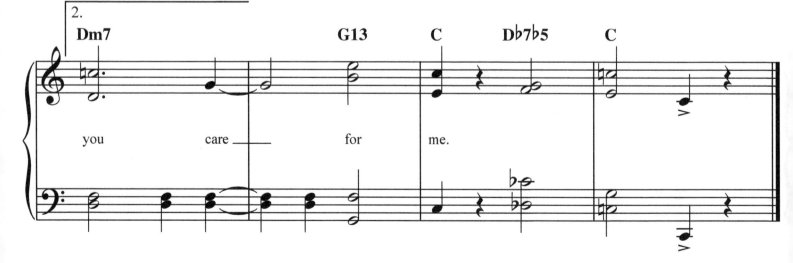

THEY CAN'T TAKE THAT AWAY FROM ME

from THE BARKLEYS OF BROADWAY

Music and Lyrics by GEORGE GERSHWIN
and IRA GERSHWIN

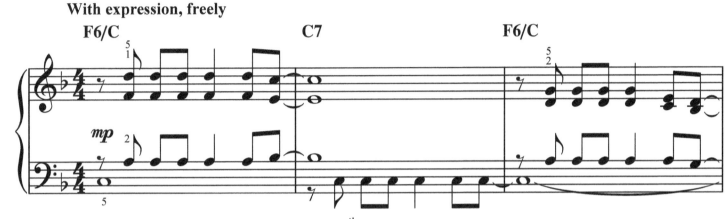

Our ro-mance won't end on a sor-row-ful

note, though by to-mor-row you're gone; the

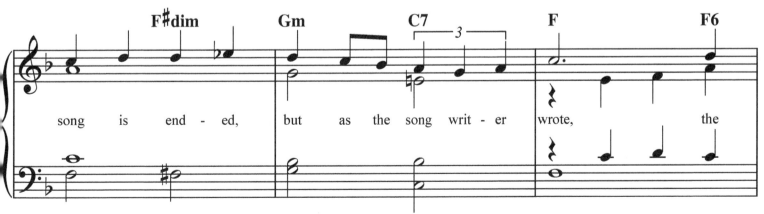

song is end-ed, but as the song writ-er wrote, the

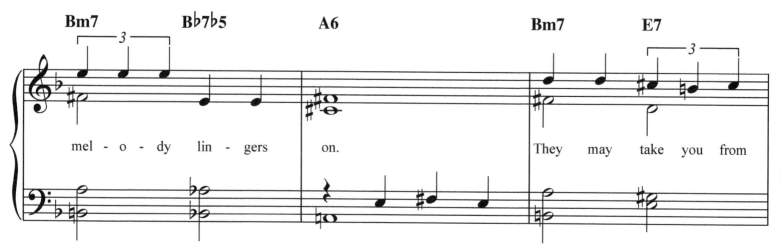

mel - o - dy lin - gers on.   They may take you from

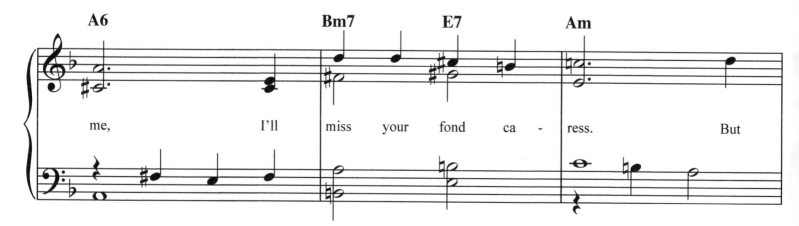

me,   I'll miss your fond ca - ress.   But

though they take you from me, I'll still po - sess:

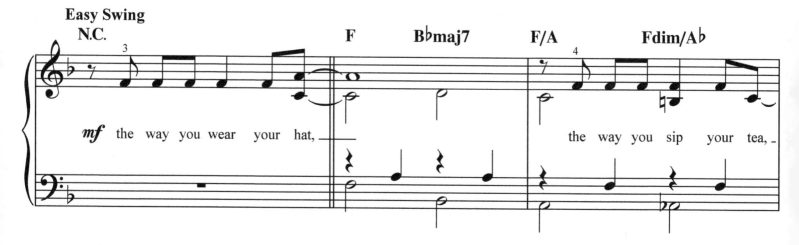

Easy Swing

mf the way you wear your hat, ___   the way you sip your tea, ___

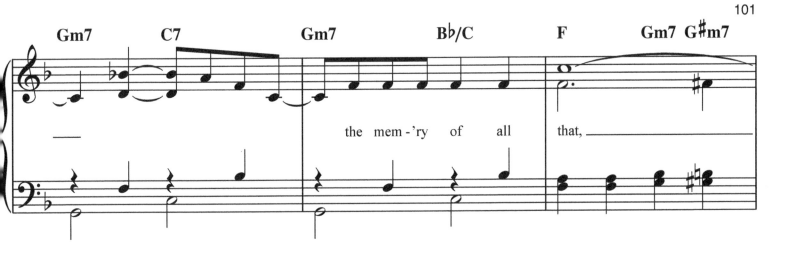

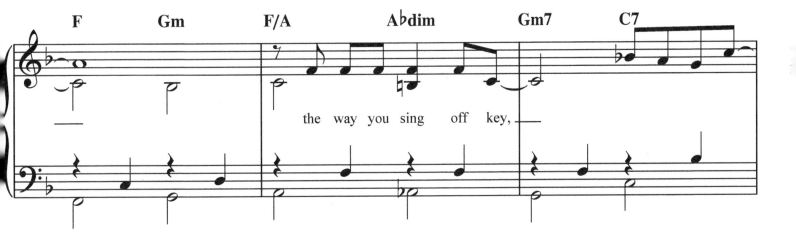

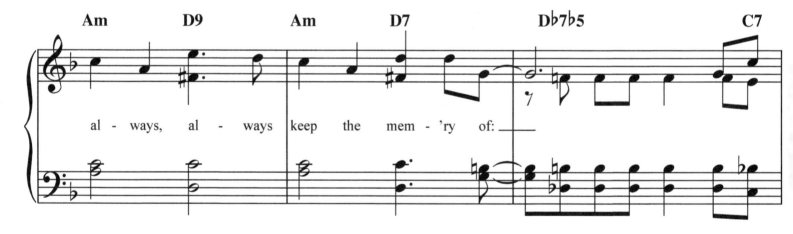

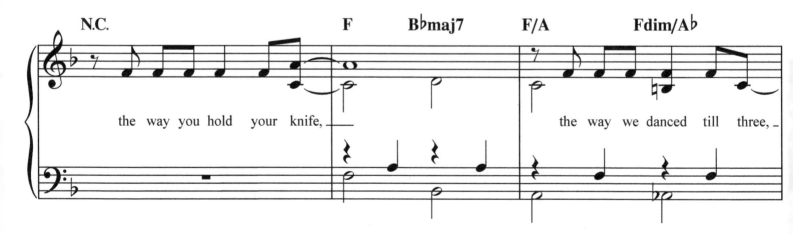

103

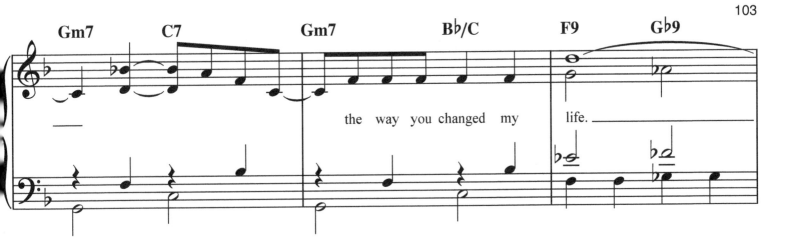

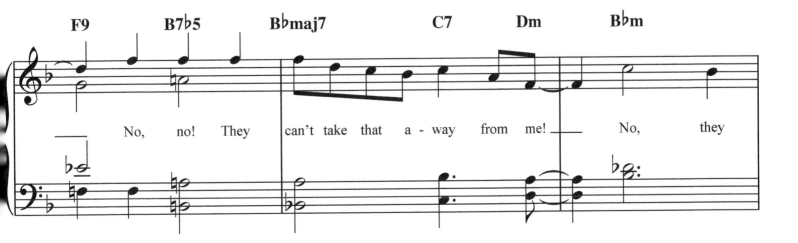

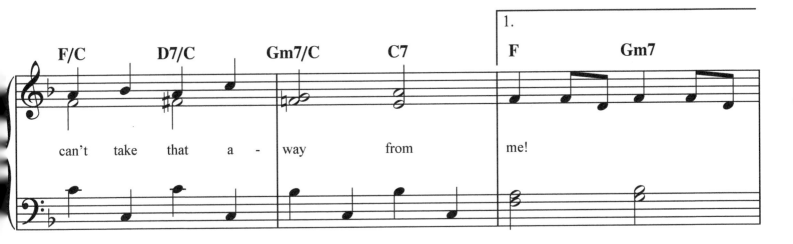

LEARN TO PLAY JAZZ PIANO

With Method Books Available from Hal Leonard

HAL LEONARD JAZZ PIANO METHOD - BOOK 1
by Mark Davis
This comprehensive and easy-to-use guide is designed for anyone interested in playing jazz piano. Topics include essential theory, chords and voicings, improvisation ideas, structure and forms, scales and modes, rhythm basics, interpreting a lead sheet, playing solos, and much more!
00131102 Book/Online Audio

HAL LEONARD JAZZ PIANO METHOD - BOOK 2
by Mark Davis
Book 2 of *The Hal Leonard Jazz Piano Method* is a detailed guide covering many harmonic concepts, useful licks, and comping techniques for you to absorb. Includes: harmonic exercises; melodic vocabulary; chord progressions and substitutions; melodic minor scale theory; locked-hands style; drop-two voicings; stride; walking bass lines; Latin styles; modern sounds; and more!
00236177 Book/Online Audio

HAL LEONARD JAZZ PIANO FOR KIDS
by Richard Michael
Kids will stay motivated as they improvise on popular children's songs arranged in a jazz style, while the opportunity to play alongside video accompaniments will inspire a love for performance. Every song seamlessly integrates a new improvisatory skill, systematically building upon previous learning and enabling the student to progress with confidence. Topics covered include: swing and syncopation • echo playing • call and response • rock and swing grooves • improvising on 1-5 notes • hearing chord changes • 12-bar blues • and more.
00319674 Book/Online Video

THE ASPIRING JAZZ PIANIST
A METHOD FOR THE SOLO & COMBO PIANIST
by Debbie Denke
This method will show you how to arrange and improvise to popular and jazz tunes in your own style, using a clear, step-by-step method. It can be used for personal instruction or as a classroom text. The audio features both solo piano demonstrations and bass and drum accompaniments that let you practice playing with a rhythm section.
00290480 Book/Online Audio

INTRO TO JAZZ PIANO
HAL LEONARD KEYBOARD STYLE SERIES
by Mark Harrison
From comping to soloing, you'll learn the theory, the tools, and the techniques used by the pros. Covers: jazz chords and progressions; jazz swing and bossa nova comping; voicings and patterns; melodic treatment; soloing techniques; how to play from a fake book; and more. Get started today!
00312088 Book/Online Audio

JAZZ BAND PIANIST
by Jeremy Siskind
A perfect primer for a middle-school or high-school age pianist interested in joining their local or school jazz ensemble, this book consists of step-by-step instruction, review exercises, and practice pieces, as well as accompanying audio featuring live jazz musicians. Through clear, unintimidating instruction and fun pieces composed by jazz pianist Jeremy Siskind, students learn how to read chord symbols, "comp," and form chord voicings.
00296925 Book/Online Audio

JAZZ PIANO
THE COMPLETE METHOD
In Association with ABRSM
This pioneering set of publications and optional assessment materials provides the building blocks you need to play jazz with imagination, understanding and style, and to improvise effectively right from the start. Within each level there are 15 pieces, aural tests, quick studies, scales, arpeggios and a CD. Each piece provides a head/melody which contains all the characteristic voicings, phrasing, and rhythmic patterns needed for a stylish performance. An improvised section follows, where guideline pitches and left-hand voicings are given as a practical starting point for solos. Totally accessible and at the highest musical standards, these pieces provide the opportunity to play jazz confidently and creatively!
00290529 Level 1 Book/CD Pack $14.99

JAZZ PIANO BASICS - BOOK 1
by Eric Baumgartner
Willis Music
Book 1 of a two-volume series that presents the fundamentals of jazz in a logical and accessible way, primarily through short progressive exercises. Concepts covered include: • Improvisation • Swing rhythms • Common jazz chords and scales • Accompaniment techniques • 12-bar blues, and much more!
00234476 Book/Online Audio

JAZZ PIANO BASICS - BOOK 2
by Eric Baumgartner
Willis Music
Book 2 explores concepts in greater depth and introduces the most important aspects of jazz theory in a style that's easy to grasp. Also useful for pianists interested in participating in a school jazz program. The online audio tracks are indispensable to the series, in particular the fun and practical Q&A improv exercises.
00234477 Book/Online Audio

100 JAZZ LESSONS
KEYBOARD LESSON GOLDMINE SERIES
by Peter Deneff & Brent Edstrom
Expand your keyboard knowledge with 100 individual modules that cover a giant array of topics including: scales, modes and progressions; Latin jazz styles; improvisation ideas; harmonic voicings; building your chops; and more. You'll also get useful tips and more to reinforce your learning experience.
00122261 Book/Online Audio

THINK JAZZ!
COMPOSER SHOWCASE SERIES
Early Intermediate Level
by Bill Boyd
Here is a thorough, inventive method especially for young students. Teachers and students with little or no prior knowledge of jazz idioms will find this book easy to follow, and will enjoy the great original songs that form the core of this informative book. Includes units on: Jazz Rhythms & Accompaniments • Basic Improvisation • Ragtime • '50s Rock • Playing from a Fake Book • Blues • Rock and Stride Bass • Boogie Woogie • and more.
00290417 Book

HAL•LEONARD®
www.halleonard.com

Prices, contents, and availability subject to change without notice.